Advancing Strategic Sourcing and Healthcare Affordability

The United States spends more than 17% of its gross domestic product (GDP) on health care, while other developed countries throughout the world average 8.7% of GDP on healthcare expenditures. By 2028, that percentage in the United States is projected to be 19.7% of GDP.

Yet all this spending apparently doesn't equate to value, quality, or performance. Among 11 high-income countries, the U.S. healthcare industry ranked last during the past seven years in four key performance categories: administrative efficiency, access to care, equity, and healthcare outcomes. This book centers on ways to bring down skyrocketing healthcare costs and improve comparatively low patient outcomes by focusing on the second-highest cost after staffing in U.S. healthcare: the supply chain. The authors present strategies for aligning the healthcare supply chain, leadership, physicians, and department budget owners to achieve evidence-based value analysis (EVA) and effective strategic sourcing. The key to bringing alignment to where it needs to be is understanding the art and science of EVA and strategic sourcing and reorienting the health systems toward productively and gainfully accomplishing them both. Within healthcare, the biggest opportunities for a quantum leap in affordability and quality directly tie to improving the product and service selection process through EVA and greatly advancing hospital and health system supply chain sourcing strategies. The book outlines what the authors call the Lacuna Triangle—three lacunas (or gaps) that occur in hospitals and health systems that prevent them from pursuing effective EVA and strategic sourcing. The authors explore the three effects of those gaps, which keep the Lacuna Triangle walls tightly closed so that the oligopolies, irrational markets, and irrational pricing that those gaps create can continue to thrive, and where many healthcare organizations remain trapped. The goal with this book is to pluck the supply chain and health system executive and clinical leadership out of the chaos and irrationality they are caught in and give them tactics and strategies for reengineering the alignment of these processes to serve their enterprises' needs.

The book does this by a deep exploration into strategic sourcing, a way of doing business that has been embraced and employed effectively for decades in supply chain management in various industries and in healthcare supply chain in other countries.

Advancing Strategic Sourcing and Healthcare Affordability
Our Discovery of the Lacuna Triangle

Michael Georgulis Jr. and Mark C. West

Forewords by Samuel A. Greco and
Michael O'Boyle

Routledge
Taylor & Francis Group

A PRODUCTIVITY PRESS BOOK

Designed cover image: TBC

First published 2025
by Routledge
605 Third Avenue, New York, NY 10158

and by Routledge
4 Park Square, Milton Park, Abingdon, Oxon, OX14 4RN

Routledge is an imprint of the Taylor & Francis Group, an informa business

Library of Congress Cataloging-in-Publication Data
Names: Georgulis, Michael, Jr., author. | West, Mark C. author.
Title: Advancing strategic sourcing and healthcare affordability : the key to unlocking the lacuna triangle / Michael Georgulis Jr. and Mark C. West.
Description: New York, NY : Routledge, 2025. | Includes bibliographical references and index.
Identifiers: LCCN 2024021772 (print) | LCCN 2024021773 (ebook) | ISBN 9781032800745 (hardback) | ISBN 9781032800738 (paperback) | ISBN 9781003495291 (ebook)
Subjects: MESH: Health Expenditures | Health Services Administration | Equipment and Supplies, Hospital—economics | Evidence-Based Practice—economics | Quality of Health Care—economics | United States
Classification: LCC RA410.53 .G465 2025 (print) | LCC RA410.53 (ebook) | NLM W 74 AA1 | DDC 338.4/73621—dc23/eng/20240705
LC record available at https://lccn.loc.gov/2024021772
LC ebook record available at https://lccn.loc.gov/2024021773

ISBN: 978-1-032-80074-5 (hbk)
ISBN: 978-1-032-80073-8 (pbk)
ISBN: 978-1-003-49529-1 (ebk)

DOI: 10.4324/9781003495291

Typeset in Galliard
by Apex CoVantage, LLC

Contents

Figures

About the Authors

Michael Georgulis Jr. has a four-decade career as a healthcare supply chain leader in health systems, group purchasing organizations, a clinical research company, and a commercial payer, including industry leaders IASIS Healthcare, HealthTrust Purchasing Group, Premier Health Alliance, and UnitedHealth Group. His experience includes international healthcare responsibilities supporting UnitedHealthcare Global's provider operations in South America and Europe. Mike's ambitions include publishing works that share his experiences with other healthcare supply chain leaders. His passion in healthcare is to provide a platform for others to better understand supply chain strategic sourcing, the medical device industry and how a lack of transparency, affordability, and quality are placing patients at risk. Mike currently works as a healthcare supply chain consultant and serves as a board member of a healthcare company.

Mark C. West has more than three decades of experience in developing and leading high-performing supply chain organizations and companies within manufacturing, aerospace, and healthcare industries. This journey has provided him the opportunity to gain wide-ranging national and international experience and perspective. The second half of his career has been within healthcare, leading Cleveland Clinic's supply chain, followed by joining UnitedHealth Group as the architect and senior officer of SharedClarity. A Self-Described "Industry Disruptor" With a Passion for Improving Healthcare Affordability and Outcomes, he coauthored this book with the intent of creating an insightful, thought-provoking, and inspiring vehicle for positive change within the healthcare industry. Currently, Mark devotes his time to entrepreneurial, consulting, and advisory activities through his private investment company.

Foreword by Samuel A. Greco

I first met Michael Georgulis when he was an associate in the Corporate Supply Chain Management Department at Columbia/HCA (now HCA Healthcare and HealthTrust Performance Group). I helped develop and establish the supply chain department concept throughout all of Columbia/HCA, and the corporate SCM department reported to me in my role of Senior Vice President of Financial Operations.

Achieving continual improvement in contracting and sourcing for a large organization is not overly difficult, so many associates followed the path that was already established and worked to provide positive results. Finding their value and exploring what is possible was often not high among their goals.

This is where Mike stood out. He was a "thinker." I recall having conversations with him about trying to find our true leverage points so we could continually reset the market and impact the company and the industry. I thought we were in a position and at a unique point in time when we could not only impact the market but also lead it. I believed our actions caused a surge in group purchasing organization (GPO) activity, but also in integrated delivery networks (IDNs) starting to act a little more independently. Mike was one of the few on the team who sought to understand how all of this worked and why it was so critical.

At the time, I was looking to differentiate our organization among other IDNs with suppliers as a highly compliant organization—that we were committed to doing what we said we were going to do. Mike was also one of the few who looked for that differentiation, aligning us with those who contributed to our quality, cost structure, and reputation. Both of these concepts—of alignment and commitment—form a vital thread throughout this book.

Addressing the Talent Gap

The talent deficit in healthcare laid out in this book is not just in supply chain management but also at the CFO and COO levels, as it relates to the supply chain issues. As the authors have outlined here, our industry needs to do a better job influencing the best and brightest to become involved in healthcare. We are behind the curve. Every other developed industry appreciates the impact of its supply chain on process, waste, meeting standards, and pursuing better and best practices. They put a premium on strong supply chain managers and leaders.

Can you think of any industry that defers its supply decisions to third parties the way some healthcare provider organizations do with GPOs and suppliers? Supply chain executives need to have a better understanding of sourcing, their options, and their natural buying leverage. They need to access all sources of information available to them—including manufacturers, distributors, and GPOs—to make more informed recommendations.

COOs and those directing services (invasive and noninvasive procedures) need to understand the process currently in place to perform and complete the service. Some COOs I've dealt with have a perception of how things are done, but they don't spend enough time truly comparing *their perception* to what is *actually being done*. As the authors cover in this book, there has to be knowledge of the variation that exists within the service performance process and with whom the variation lies. From there, leaders can take control and be the catalyst for improvement—assessing current, better, and best practice standards, and then implementing them.

Putting the Right People in the Right Places

While we're comparing our practices with others, can you think of any other industry that does not involve the individual who knows the most about a significant portion of cost in the growth process? I would suggest that too few who have the talent at the healthcare COO and supply chain manager levels participate in the process of selecting high-cost, physician preference items (PPIs), such as implants. As an industry we spend more time and money on revenue cycle management than we do on productivity and supply chain impact yet omit margin management from this process. This results in situations in which, say, a Medicaid case ends up being reimbursed for a complete knee replacement at below the cost of the device. What other industry would do that?

Virtually, every reimbursement rate now is prospective. So, cost management is critical. Even COOs to a large extent have limited control over labor costs in the operating room or the cardiac cath lab, given today's labor challenges. In many cases, COOs also have little knowledge of what products are on the physician preference cards, or what the cost of an implant is, so they're not sure of the supply cost. And the one very controllable cost in all of this is the cost of supplies; thus, the supply chain manager becomes far more critical.

For better or worse, C-suite status comes with implied knowledge and actual authority. For this reason, the individual responsible for the second-largest expense area in the health system should have both the authority to speak for the organization and lead it toward improvement. And they should have the capability to carry that responsibility to success. It must be a senior, effective manager who is willing to study and be well prepared and is respected in this field. This is a must for success.

The last technology systems that healthcare provider organizations invest in are those impacting the supply chain and cost management, and even when some are in place, some are driven by the charge/revenue systems.

I led the supply chain efforts for the largest for-profit healthcare provider organization in the nation, and at the time, I had little or no information. Often, we used sample data on Excel spread sheets to make decisions, and the supplier *always* had more and better data on our history than we did. There was little internally driven visibility, and collaboration with suppliers was generally about volume, price, and savings from the previous contract/year.

The theory of "the more you buy the more you save" was, and in many cases is still, the standard. Consumption knowledge and control, was up to some other area of the organization. So, affordability of a product should also be coupled with affordability of the service line. Is it profitable? Can it be?

Visibility into both the supply chain issues and the current practice compared to a standard is an issue when an organization approaches each service line with the perspective of profitability, safety, quality, and the patient experience.

The time has come for a book like this. In fact, it is overdue.

A Novel Foundation for Supply Chain Management

I teach the business of healthcare at the University of Oklahoma, covering healthcare economics, supply chain, marketing, operations, and administration. In 2023, I introduced the first book by Michael Georgulis and

Mark C. West, titled, *Implantable Medical Devices and Affordability: Exposing the Spiderweb* to my healthcare supply chain course students.

I believe my students in this program will benefit from *Advancing Strategic Sourcing and Healthcare Affordability: Our Discovery of the Lacuna Triangle* even more than they did from the first book.

That being said, I would introduce this book in two or three of my courses beyond supply chain, because I believe it is well suited to anyone in the healthcare organization who is responsible for operations at all levels. This includes chief operations officers, chief supply chain management officers (in organizations where that position exists), product line managers, and even clinical and surgical directors.

The system of evidence-based value analysis combined with effective strategic sourcing that Mike and Mark propose in this book is a novel and long-needed approach. Like the majority of those associates I mentioned above, in general, we repeat what has been done in the past, looking for some higher level of savings and then declaring victory. But some do this without the benefit of research into real historical volumes and costs. Some also completely defer their decisions to a group purchasing organization (GPO), which will always seek the "highest low price" from multiple sources to protect their revenue stream—a practice that is examined in detail in this book.

An evidence-based approach will require more involvement by knowledgeable clinical, financial, and process professionals than is usual. I agree, as these authors point out, that in many of our health systems we simply do not currently have the talent to achieve this goal. Still, I believe if we start diligently working on that goal, the talent will begin to develop naturally out of necessity.

Even if these efforts do nothing more than identifying savings opportunities and expose waste, we would be far ahead of where we are now. However, knowing what to do is one thing, but having the authority to act once we do know is quite another. This is where the talent gap and the lack of C-suite presence addressed in this book come in.

Who Will Benefit from This Book?

Anyone who leads operations at all levels in the healthcare provider organization and anyone who wishes to become a valuable member of their management team should read this book. I would love to see CEOs spend more time reading something like this. A good CEO would benefit because they all want their teams to be better.

The following are some of the people in critical positions who I believe will benefit from this book along with some of its related takeaways.

Chief Operations Officers. Understanding the operations of a healthcare enterprise includes understanding customers (and healthcare has many), service/product lines, and the various prices we are paid for services from different sources. Part of understanding operations is also having knowledge of the cost of the service offered and overall profitability. Margin management cannot be achieved without this knowledge. Quality of the service and the products included in those services should be a requirement. Thus, the variation among surgeons/clinicians must be understood, including patient safety, real documented outcomes, and costs attributed to their PPIs.

Chief Supply Chain Management Officers. First and foremost, the person in this C-suite level position must be a cost manager, understanding the costs of each procedure, and the variation among physicians and their PPIs. They should be a part of the team evaluating product/service lines, and that team must have knowledge of the payer mix. They must be the primary educator in the enterprise when it comes to PPIs and their impact. They need to know the market—the high and low pricing, GPO options, and where the organization lands in the market and where it should be.

Product Line Managers. These leaders should understand all aspects of their product/service lines. They should have real data on the performance of physicians, not only financially but in terms of safety, patient experience, and outcomes.

Clinical and Surgical Directors. These leaders can be the eyes and ears of an organization from a supply chain management perspective. They see and hear the positive and negative from clinicians, surgeons, and surgical personnel. The need to be aware of best and better practices to continually elevate performance.

By nature of where they work in health systems and their potential impact, supply chain managers should be better compensated, and the value of their voices should be elevated, as they are in the type of system described in this book.

CFOs and CEOs generally can't speak supply. I have encountered many COOs whose real aspiration is to be a CEO and who are focused mainly on the top line. If you can put together an understanding of people/process/technology as it relates to these supplies, that is powerful, because it encompasses all of the other existential issues of safety, quality, outcomes, patient experience, and more.

When a health system is looking for a new COO, a supply chain manager who has been developed and empowered in the manner laid out in this book should be the most likely COO candidate. They can speak product and process. They can speak finance. They can speak doctor. They understand how to drive improvement throughout the organization.

This book lays out a system for helping not only supply chain managers but all of the stakeholders in the value chain meet and overcome many of the pressing cost and outcome challenges of health systems and U.S. healthcare as a whole.

As I said before, a book like this is overdue. It should serve to inspire the current and future crop of not only supply chain managers but of all who aspire to higher positions in the organization and care about our healthcare system.

Samuel A. Greco
Senior Instructor for the Business of Healthcare at the
University of Oklahoma, Price College of Business
Former Senior Vice President of
Financial Operations for Columbia/HCA

Foreword by Michael O'Boyle

To say that I fully agree with the observations of Mark C. West and Michael Georgulis in this book would be an understatement. For too long, the value of supply chain management in general, and strategic sourcing in particular, has been underrecognized, understated, and underappreciated in healthcare. The authors have gone about isolating, identifying, and addressing the major issues currently facing healthcare delivery in the United States and then presenting solutions through the lens of their expertise—the supply chain. I fully believe in, and endorse, the combination of evidence-based value analysis and strategic sourcing presented by Mark and Michael as a significant means of addressing the out-of-control costs and underwhelming outcomes that are produced in our system today.

Why Do I Believe This?

Because I've seen it work. With substantial management support and the collaboration of physician leadership, Mark and I made it happen together in the real world at Cleveland Clinic. A few years later, with Michael's help, success was realized again at UnitedHealthcare, this time through a joint venture with four major health systems called SharedClarity. The organizations not only improved their cost profile, but they also drove physician consensus regarding instrumentation and device specifications and performance, rationalized suppliers, and helped eliminate opinion in favor of evidence, thus enhancing outcomes.

To better appreciate the passion these authors feel about the importance of the supply chain in healthcare and the need for change, one has to understand some of the history regarding the evolution of our current system of care delivery.

Costs, Consolidations, and Complications

Leading into the 1980s, healthcare was largely thought to be a cottage industry, populated by small to medium-sized hospitals as the main delivery engines. As enterprises, they were mostly not-for-profit, community or academically based, and singularly incorporated and aligned. The evolution into the large, sophisticated, multijurisdictional systems of care that we experience today was in its infancy.

It was a time of principally cost-based reimbursement, and it was dominated by Blue Cross plans, Medicare, and Medicaid. Any financial margin was derived from the very small percentage of patients that were either covered by commercial carriers or were self-responsible. The major independent commercial insurers that we know today were virtually nonexistent or irrelevant in most markets. Hospital reimbursement generally came in the form of periodic interim payments received from the various payers throughout the year, validated and reconciled at year-end through the filing of annual cost reports.

As for physicians, most were either engaged in private practice or were employed by a sponsoring academic institution. Upon acceptance of a formal application, physicians were granted privileges to practice at one or more hospitals. Hospitals were not compensated for granting these privileges. Because they were compensated by the insurer or the patient directly in the form of fees for their services, and because they did not pay the hospital for the privilege to practice there, they had little or no economic ties to those organizations. Since hospitals were paid on the basis of costs, and physicians were independently paid a fee for their service, there was a rational contention across government and employers that costs were continuously increasing at alarming and unsupportable rates because there was no incentive to control them.

This situation of ever-increasing costs began to be addressed directly in the mid-1980s as Medicare moved to fixed-price payments for hospital-based inpatient services. As this transition took hold and was adopted by most major Blue Cross plans, my contemporaries were forced to become much more invested in improving cost performance. When further magnified through the creation of managed care and health maintenance organizations, our hospitals' economic health became compromised.

As most of our organizations were smaller in size and scale, we had very limited bargaining power with those that supplied us with the goods and services necessary to sustain our delivery engines. This included instrumentation, implantable devices, monitors, sophisticated diagnostic machinery, and pharmaceuticals, all of which materially drove our cost base. The formation of group purchasing organizations (GPOs) emerged as a way for us to join forces and theoretically provide better pricing, availability, and distribution for the benefit of the patients we served.

While the role and importance of the GPO were growing, hospitals and other providers of care began to band together to form systems of care delivery to create size, scale, and sophistication that would help provide further negotiating leverage with suppliers and insurers. Speaking of which, proprietary insurers also developed and expanded during this time, challenging the long dominant position of the Blue Cross plans in many markets.

With the evolution of health systems, the growth in importance of the GPOs, and the development of new insurance—and therefore payment—models, the late 1980s and 1990s were a period of profound change in the industry. Complicating matters further, the role and structure of physician practices were also transforming as doctors reacted to the changing landscape of hospital organizations and the increasing influence of new payers. They formed practice groups, some of which were multispecialty and some of which were single specialty in nature. They provided clinical guidance to the GPOs, sometimes through sponsoring hospitals or health systems and sometimes independently. And they also provided research, education, and scientific support to manufacturers, suppliers, and pharmaceutical companies in exchange for honoraria, consulting contracts, and other forms of compensation. And to further blur the lines of alignment and/or create controversy, where their participation led to patents or other scientific discoveries, they could also receive licensing fees or royalties.

One can easily see how this unhealthy amalgam of events created a very uneven, irrational, confusing, complicated, and conflicting state of affairs that afflicts our healthcare delivery system to this day.

An Irrational Evolution Takes Hold

As the authors reference, it is under this irrational system that physician preferences evolved. They developed outside the scope of the GPO, and despite efforts to the contrary, the two never aligned. Boiling it all down, you had four major influences happening simultaneously, all of which challenged the notion that healthcare in the United States could be delivered efficiently and effectively:

■ The evolution of various and highly conflicting arrangements with payment mechanisms for physicians

- The development of health systems and payer enterprises whose incentives are in outright conflict
- The movement from cost-based reimbursement to unfamiliar, complicated, and highly variable payment mechanisms
- The establishment and growing influence of GPOs that were reluctant to cede the power and authority they acquired and nurtured.

Consequently, the supply chain space never progressed in a manner that would allow it to influence behavior and performance as it did in other industries. We placed too much reliance on the GPOs and thereby did not develop our internal capabilities like we should have. As the authors correctly point out, the lack of advancement and maturation of the supply chain discipline manifested itself in three different ways:

1. A talent gap and training deficit
2. A sometimes blind acceptance of physician preference items
3. A lack of strategic alignment among the affected parties.

Despite the best intentions of all the parties involved, this was precisely the situation at the Cleveland Clinic in the late 1990s and early 2000s.

Moving Toward Evidence-Based Value Analysis and Strategic Sourcing

The 1990s had generally been a time of great prosperity for the Cleveland Clinic, with major new facilities and enhanced programs on its main campus, the development of a regional health system in Northeast Ohio, and expansion into Florida with new hospitals and clinics in two different markets. At the same time, the Clinic had become too dependent on investment assets as its financial underpinning and its performance from operations suffered. With the downturn in the financial markets in the late 1990s and operations underperforming, the Clinic's long-term viability was challenged. There was an immediate need to reverse direction and have the operations become the engine of prosperity and growth, augmented by investments, as opposed to vice versa as had been the case. With the complete and unwavering support of Clinic leadership, we embarked on a journey to refocus the organization. Part of this journey included revamping the Clinic's supply chain management, and this led me to Mark C. West.

Generally speaking, the largest operating cost component of any healthcare delivery organization is labor. Following that are the costs associated with supply chain. The Clinic was no exception. Given its size and scale, the opportunities were many and included inventory management and distribution, order processing, GPO relationships, and contracting.

Following a thorough review of our systems and exposure, we decided to tackle high-value, controllable items first. Thus, our energies were directed at our GPO relationships and the evaluation and sourcing of high-cost, high-use critical instrumentation and devices. Under Mark's leadership, we brought a value-analysis approach commonly used in other industries to move away from the notion of preference and toward evidence-based decision-making. This process was uncommon in the industry at that time and severely challenged accepted norms.

Regardless of the industry and the issues being addressed, change management is hard work. It requires commitment, patience, and persistence. In this instance we were addressing issues, style, and culture that permeated not only in a world-renowned organization but also an entire industry for years and years. Any time an outsider brought new and different ways of doing things to the table, the prevailing mantra was, "You don't understand healthcare—we're different." In many ways, there is some truth to this. Healthcare is different in nuance by its many design features, by behaviors that became accepted norms over the years, and by the dysfunction that arose from the misaligned incentives described earlier. That said, at its core, the industry is still about finding ways to provide the most effective care to the individual upon whom the entire system is based—the patient.

Despite the difficulty in changing behavior ingrained in a process over many years, no one could factually argue the benefits of evidence-based evaluation and strategic sourcing of materials used to provide the best possible care of and outcomes for the patient. To do this, we had to convince world-class physicians to abandon some of their old ways of thinking and, in some cases, their competing individual interests and introduce new approaches common in other industries.

To effectively manage this change and achieve our goals of lower costs, more uniform practices, and better outcomes, we had to do the following:

■ Obtain the full and unwavering commitment of the organization's leadership, as no matter how careful and thoughtful the process, there would be those who would find fault and become obstructive.

- Put physicians at the center of decision-making. As the ones being asked to change behavior, they needed to make the key decisions.
- Include other relevant and important parties in the process: legal, risk management, compliance, technology, etc. This is necessary to not only address key issues but to bring alignment across disciplines.
- Address the process in manageable bites, selecting categories and items where change is doable and impactful.
- Bring credible, evidence-based data and analysis to the table, such that opinion-based preferences are eliminated.
- Have a competent, experienced supply chain team that can turn decisions into demonstrated reality such that caregivers come to trust the process.

In the case of Cleveland Clinic, this approach yielded annual, recurring savings of more than $100 million. The results were proven and the process repetitive. That said, to my knowledge, there's no textbook that can tell you how to align physicians' interests and practices with those of the underlying organization. There's no great magic in what we did, but there is magic in the word "we." It took Mark's knowledge and expertise, the belief and support of the C-suite, and physician leaders and practitioners who were willing to coalesce around the goal of better care for patients and better results for the organization.

In later years, I moved on to a position with UnitedHealthcare, leading their network enterprise, comprising 5,000+ hospitals, 650,000 physicians, and many hundreds of ancillary providers. A different challenge for sure, but one which provided another opportunity to harness the power of evidence-based value analysis and strategic sourcing. In this case, we questioned whether the efforts of hospitals and health systems couldn't be enhanced if we introduced the buying power and data capabilities of a major insurer.

Once again, I turned to Mark C. West to lead these efforts. Along with Michael Georgulis and the collaboration of wonderful colleagues from Dignity Health, we undertook another effort to introduce major change in the healthcare supply chain arena. A joint venture called "SharedClarity" was formed to engage in the process, and we were eventually joined by three other major health systems. SharedClarity provided the means to merge payer (claims) data and health system data into meaningful outcomes intelligence. It evolved from a business model to a plan supported by two major players to an operational launch with several other investors. It was yet another attempt to bring collaboration and alignment to a system of disjointed partners for the greater good of the patient and the organizations involved.

In this book, the authors take you on a journey that begins by laying out some of the challenges faced by our healthcare system and ends by providing solutions to some of those challenges. They provide recommendations to upgrade the caliber and capabilities of supply chain management along with an introduction to evidence-based value analysis and strategic sourcing. And they introduce the attributes necessary to navigate this journey, including effective communication, dedication to the process of change, a collaborative mindset, executive involvement, business acumen, and data analysis.

I wholeheartedly endorse their recommendations and approach. As I said earlier, I've seen it work firsthand. Anyone involved in the business of healthcare will enjoy reading this book.

Michael O'Boyle
Retired CEO of Ventra Health
Former COO and CFO of Cleveland Clinic

Preface

Advancing Strategic Sourcing and Healthcare Affordability

We have spent a lot of time getting to this point.

From 2010 through 2019, 37 of the 38 countries in the Organisation for Economic Co-operation and Development (OECD), excluding the United States, spent an average of 8.7% of their GDP on healthcare, and none of even the richest countries on the list ever got much above 10% in any of those years. During the same period, the United States went from spending 16.3% of its GDP on healthcare to spending 17%. Worse, you have to go all the way back to 1979—four decades—to find a year in which U.S. healthcare spending was less than 8.7% of its GDP. And things are not improving. By 2028, the Centers for Medicare and Medicaid Services (CMS) projects U.S. healthcare spending will be 19.6% of GDP.

But it's worth it because we have the best clinical outcomes in the entire world, right?

Wrong. As we will detail in Chapter 1, all of this burdensome spending does not result in better outcomes for patients, and in fact, our health outcomes in key areas—little things like life expectancy, infant mortality, unaddressed diabetes, maternal mortality, and much more—are among the worst in the developed world.

These trends are unacceptable and unsustainable. They are destined to cripple the progress of our nation for the generations that come after us. It is going to take a lot of work to get us out of this mess, and that is what this book is about. We believe much of it is fixable if we focus on the second highest cost center after staffing (and arguably soon to become the highest) of health system business—the supply chain—and use lessons from other industries and healthcare systems in other countries.

In this book we also lend our own experience developing winning approaches to healthcare supply chain management, specifically in evidence-based value analysis (EVA) and strategic sourcing. Together, we have nearly 70 years in the supply chain profession and more than 50 years in the healthcare industry, including experience within the largest commercial payer (UnitedHealthcare), world-renowned health systems (Cleveland Clinic and UnitedHealthcare Global), the most influential healthcare group purchasing organization (Premier Health Alliance), and an unprecedented joint venture (SharedClarity).

Our first book, *Implantable Medical Devices and Healthcare Affordability: Exposing the Spiderweb*, presented the implantable medical device (IMD) sub-ecosystem of the healthcare supply chain as a prime lesson for detailing the challenges in healthcare affordability and outcomes that occur throughout the entire U.S. healthcare industry. And we detailed how these challenges are allowed to grow and fester. We chose that segment of the industry because it is a microcosm of greater supply chain issues in which U.S. health systems pay up to six times more for some IMDs than their counterparts do in Europe, and prices for the same IMD model vary widely even among various U.S. hospitals and health systems. We exposed the IMD Spiderweb, as we call it, as a place where physicians, health system CEOs, group purchasing organizations, health insurance companies, and supply chain executives are ensnared for the benefit of only one player.

In this book we zoom out to a much wider view that encompasses not only the entire healthcare supply chain but also the other areas of the health system enterprise that are impacted by decisions made there. We demonstrate how components of health systems and their leadership need to align to meet the challenge of runaway costs and poor health outcomes for their ultimate customers, both internal and external. As we did in the first book, we provide insights into all the participants, and how they interact, but on a much broader scale. We show how the ecosystem that has been created damages affordability, transparency, quality, and the ability for anyone inside or outside the enterprise to get reliable outcomes data.

This book explores the status and maturity of current supply chain management/strategic sourcing in relation to the aforementioned challenges. We compare and contrast the healthcare supply chain in the United States with those in other countries and in industries outside healthcare, sharing lessons applicable to our current systems along the way. The book details how leaders can adjust their supply chain and strategic sourcing strategies, relationships, and resources to achieve a quantum leap in affordability and outcomes comparable to results in other industries and countries. An entire section of this book is dedicated to advanced strategies for achieving these aims.

We believe we have provided a well-researched and thoroughly considered argument on the urgent need for change in the way the healthcare supply chain operates within health system and hospital enterprises. We have presented scenarios for your consideration that we hope will lead to positive disruption and the development of individuals who might view themselves as change agents—leading necessary new directions, thoughts, and practices in the healthcare supply chain discipline.

With this work we intend to inform, educate, and coach current and future healthcare supply chain leaders by communicating practical, tried, and tested approaches to EVA and strategic sourcing. We encourage health systems to pilot our suggested supply chain management and strategic sourcing changes, and we offer ourselves as a resource to the industry.

Dedications and Acknowledgments

I dedicate this work to my wonderful, loving family. To my father, Michael Georgulis Sr., and my mother, Joan Hill-Georgulis, who lived a blessed marriage life together prior to passing in recent years. Also, to my siblings, Karyn Georgulis-Reschke, Sandra Georgulis-Ihrig, and Mark Edward Georgulis, all whom I love dearly.

I want to acknowledge my incredible experience at Columbia/HCA under the leadership of Rick Scott, the CEO of the company, while I was employed there during the mid to late 1990s. My specific mention is Samuel Greco, who was the senior vice president of financial operations for Columbia/HCA and led supply chain for the entire company of approximately 450 hospitals nationwide. Sam influenced my supply chain and strategic sourcing development in ways that neither I nor he could have imagined at the time. I'm sincerely grateful for his thoughtful, seasoned, and knowledgeable mentorship and leadership during this time in my professional development.

Michael Georgulis Jr.

I dedicate this work to my wife Juli and our sons Tyler and Maxwell, for their love and support during my career, which at times included extensive travel, while effectively juggling their own education and careers.

I want to acknowledge Cleveland Clinic for facilitating my entry into the healthcare industry and providing me the opportunity to lead and reengineer their supply chain using best practices from inside and outside healthcare. I could not have accomplished so much without support from visionary leaders that included Michael O'Boyle, Dr. Kenneth Ouriel, Dr. Delos "Toby" Cosgrove, and Dr. Joseph Hahn.

Mark C. West

Introduction

What happens in the U.S. healthcare system today is well below the standard of what strategic sourcing should be in our industry and how it exists in other industries and other healthcare systems around the world. In American healthcare, costs remain high and grow higher every year, becoming a greater share of our GDP, while health outcomes significantly lag those in peer countries. The supply chain is the second highest cost in American healthcare after staffing (and may soon overtake it), so we believe it offers our greatest opportunity for turning those numbers in a positive direction outside of resorting to workforce reductions.

Alignment on sourcing occurs in some hospitals and health systems, but generally speaking, it is anything but strategic, and it is in large part relinquished to the control of others. We drove this point home repeatedly in *Implantable Medical Devices and Healthcare Affordability: Exposing the Spiderweb*, released in 2023. In that book we focused narrowly on uncovering the failings of one sector of the healthcare supply chain that is emblematic of our runaway costs and poor outcomes relative to healthcare globally and unmasking the spider in that web.

In this book we switch our emphasis to strategic sourcing and alignment of the healthcare supply chain, leadership, physicians, and department budget owners with a focus on achieving evidence-based value analysis (EVA) and effective strategic sourcing. The key to bringing alignment to where it needs to be is understanding the art and science of EVA and strategic sourcing and reorienting the organization toward productively and gainfully accomplishing them both. Within healthcare the biggest opportunities for a quantum leap in affordability and quality directly tie to improving the product selection process through EVA and greatly advancing the sourcing strategies.

DOI: 10.4324/9781003495291-1

Most healthcare organizations either believe they are practicing effective EVA and strategic sourcing in-house, or they believe some other entity is handling it just fine for them. Many of them are mistaken. Few healthcare enterprises are conducting EVA and strategic sourcing well, and that is the intended primary audience for this book—people in organizations who are not realizing the true benefits of aligning around strategic sourcing. Again, many of those people believe someone else is performing EVA and strategic sourcing effectively for them, and since they are paying good money for those services, they might as well let them do their jobs while they focus on other things. We intend to challenge these assertions in this book, demonstrate the damage they are doing to healthcare organizations and the system, and show how their effects can be turned around.

We will outline what we are branding as the Lacuna Triangle—three lacunas (or gaps) that occur in hospitals and health systems that prevent them from pursuing effective EVA and strategic sourcing. We will also explore the three effects of those gaps, which keep the Lacuna Triangle tightly closed so that the oligopolies, irrational markets, and irrational pricing that those gaps create can continue to thrive within its walls, where many healthcare organizations remain trapped.

Following the Flow of This Story

We want healthcare providers to be aware of the issues and opportunities in effective strategic sourcing and value analysis activities and encourage them to be self-reliant in these efforts.

In Chapter 1, we begin by laying out the challenges in the U.S. healthcare system of high costs and poor health outcomes, which make it an outlier relative to other high-income countries around the world. We look at the major role the much higher prices of goods and services, along with the relatively higher utilization, in our system play in our outlier status. The importance of the supply chain in healthcare is presented, and we introduce a case for the supply chain management department as a starting point for meeting the challenges of high costs and poor health outcomes.

In Chapter 2, our focus shifts to the strategic sourcing model, its evolution, its scope of responsibilities, and examples of organizations that have found success with it. Necessary elements of enterprise alignment around strategic sourcing are presented, along with the role of the EVA/strategic sourcing group in its processes. Category strategies are introduced along with how they relate to creating organized and synchronized relationships among internal customers and outside suppliers.

Chapter 3 addresses how what most people see as EVA/strategic sourcing is conducted in healthcare, contrasted with the model we presented in the previous chapter, and how the differences impede effective consolidation, rationalization, and standardization activities. The role of group purchasing organizations (GPOs) and their agreements play in creating and exacerbating these challenges is detailed.

In Chapter 4, we outline three major lacunas (gaps or unfilled spaces) that impede the healthcare enterprise's ability to conduct effective EVA and strategic sourcing, as we introduce what we call "The Lacuna Triangle." These three major points of disengagement—a talent disadvantage, blind acceptance of physician preference items, and lack of strategic alignment—are detailed, along with their deleterious effects, which misdirect leverage from healthcare enterprises and uses it against them.

Chapter 5 is all about strategic alignment, starting with detailing four foundational elements of a best practice EVA/strategic sourcing model: rigorous, evidence-based value analysis processes, category strategies, supplier business reviews, and physician research. This includes infusing a category strategy mindset into the healthcare enterprise, the value of EVA leadership, and the skillset required for effective strategic sourcing.

In Chapter 6, we present advanced strategies in strategic sourcing and EVA. One of those is the Earned Price Model, which is critical in satisfying mutual interests among buyers and suppliers in negotiations and through the life of a contract. Another important advanced strategy is advancing the relationship and becoming a customer of choice with suppliers. We also address implementing contracts in a way that deters suppliers from interfering behind the scenes, removing physician preference items as a "category" by having physicians lead EVA initiatives, and how strategic sourcing professionals become the stewards of rational supply markets.

Chapter 7 delves into measuring and demonstrating the effects of strategic sourcing efforts and validating supply chain performance by a number of means, including common key performance indicators (KPIs) used in the healthcare industry. We present those but also suggest two of our own categories of KPIs that are missing from these common metrics— Realized Cost Savings and Employee Experience and Development. We contrast our method of cost-saving validation with practices that are common in today's healthcare supply chain environment.

We close with Chapter 8, where we address the future of healthcare strategic sourcing, starting with the premise of self-reliance, encouraging healthcare enterprises to take responsibility for their own strategic sourcing. We emphasize the use of an EVA process that is a physician-led effort with finance, clinical, supply chain, and the C-suite represented. This is backed up with a comprehensive strategic sourcing process with rigorous cost validation. At the end, the book comes back to alignment, which is the stream that courses throughout the book.

Where This Book Is Moving

Costs remain high, quality remains low, and alignment on EVA and strategic sourcing is somewhere in that stream, under the control of others. A supply chain operating in the optimal environment of alignment we will present in this book can be compared to a deep, vibrant river, flowing along within its long-established course, impervious to even the most aggressive outside forces and able to bounce back into its original course even in the aftermath of disastrous tumult.

Unfortunately, in the current American healthcare climate, the supply chain has burst its banks, and its alignment has been obliterated by outside forces that are intentionally capturing and controlling their directions away from the supply chain's primary objective of serving the internal financial, quality, and clinical needs of the healthcare enterprise.

Our goal is to pluck the supply chain and their leadership out of the chaos, out of the irrationality, out of that current they are caught in, dry them off, and give them tactics and strategies for reengineering the alignment of that stream to where it needs to be to serve their enterprise's needs. In other words, showing them how to get their power back, instead of letting an outside influence dictate where the alignment lies. We do this by a deep exploration into strategic sourcing, a way of doing business that has been embraced and employed effectively for decades in supply chain management in various industries and in healthcare supply chain in other countries.

We hope to encourage, enlighten, and enable you along the way.

Chapter 1

Healthcare Challenges and the Supply Chain

Before the spring of 2020, the term "healthcare supply chain" was not something that crossed the mind of the average person. Until then, in fact, there were likely a majority of professionals in healthcare that gave it little thought. Whether as a patient, a clinician, a janitor, or a lab tech, the healthcare supply chain just hums along in the background and delivers the goods and services you need when you need them.

Until it doesn't.

That is, until patients needlessly die because they could not get a ventilator or a treatment drug. That is, until a nurse contracts COVID-19 and has to stop working (or worse, dies) because what used to be a single-use item of personal protective equipment (PPE) became a two-week-use item and finally failed.

Such events woke the public up to the importance of the supply chain in healthcare. To a degree, it also created a realization in the minds of leaders in healthcare, but only because they were caught with their PPEs down. So, in the usual reactionary fashion in healthcare, they went right to work on solving some of those publicly visible and embarrassing problems. And to their credit, they have done some good.

1.1 Getting to the Heart of Supply Chain Issues

It is time to look under the gowns and gloves and behind the masks to get at the real issues plaguing the industry. The supply chain in healthcare is the second biggest expense behind staffing, and some argue it will soon become the biggest. For that reason alone, it must be taken more seriously.

In July 2023, Gartner released its "Supply Chain Top 25 for 2023," a respected gauge of best-performing organizational supply chains. The 2023 report actually also lists the 26 through 50 top supply chains. It is notable that there are no health systems in the list, even though many health systems are larger in terms of revenue and have more extensive supply chain structures than many of the organizations on the list. Neither were any healthcare GPOs in that list even though they will tell us they have supply chain and strategic sourcing operations. There are, however, about 10 organizations in that list of 50 that are suppliers for health systems.

This brings us to the bigger picture of the healthcare supply chain beyond what was laid bare to the public back in 2020 and what this book is about.

For two decades at least, healthcare leaders have been talking about something that has evolved into the concept now simply described as "value-based care." One of the most succinct definitions in the research we have found for this is: "Value in health care is the measured improvement in a person's health outcomes for the cost of achieving that improvement" (Teisberg et al., 2020).

If you take that definition out of the context of healthcare and into retail or service industries, it basically says the same thing: "Give the customer the best product or service in a given category at the cost they are willing to bear for that level of quality and reliability."

Notice that in neither of those definitions is the word "price" mentioned because "cost" goes so much deeper than price, as we will detail in this book. Also, in those definitions, the terms "best product" and "improvement in a person's health outcomes" are purely subjective based on the evaluation of the consumer, rather than being defined by the provider of the goods or services.

So, in introducing the greater environment in which the healthcare supply chain operates, let's start with cost.

1.2 Costs and Outcomes: The U.S. Healthcare System as an Outlier

As we reported in our first book, based on the OECD 2020 Health Statistics, the United States far outspent the 37 other OECD member countries in health expenditures both in percentage of GDP and in dollars spent per capita. At that time, it was reported that between 2010 and 2019, all of the other 37 OECD countries averaged 8.7% of their GDP on healthcare expenditures, while during the same period U.S. healthcare spending rose from 16.3% to approximately 17% of GDP. This means that the United States spent approximately $11,000 per capita on healthcare. The closest country at that time to the United States was Switzerland, which had $7,700 in per capita healthcare spending, which is 30% lower than in the United States (OECD, 2020).

These numbers and comparisons are not getting any better for the United States since our first book, even in the aftermath of the coronavirus pandemic, according to an analysis of the OECD 2022 Health Statistics from the Peter G. Peterson Foundation. Because, generally, wealthier countries "will spend more on healthcare than countries that are less affluent," the researchers measured U.S. healthcare spending against 12 other comparatively wealthy countries in the OECD. "Comparatively wealthy countries" are defined as those having GDP and per capita GDP above the mean of all 38 countries (Peter G. Peterson Foundation, 2022).

Among the researchers' findings are the following:

▪ In 2021, annual per capita healthcare spending in the United States was up to $12,318. The next closest OECD comparatively wealthy country was Germany, which spent $7,383 per person—only 60% of what the United States spends per capita.
▪ The average per capita healthcare expenditures of comparatively wealthy OECD countries in 2021 (excluding the United States) were $5,829—only 47% of what the United States spends per person on healthcare.
▪ Per capita administrative costs in U.S. healthcare ($1,055) are more than three times those in the closest comparatively wealthy country (Germany at $306) and five times the average of the other 12 wealthy countries ($194).

And the spending will continue to grow and take a bigger bite out of American productivity. According to the Centers for Medicare and Medicaid Services (CMS), from 2022 through 2031, healthcare spending in the United States is expected to grow an average of 5.4% per year, from 17.4% to 19.6% of GDP at the end of that period. During that time, average personal (out-of-pocket) healthcare expenditures are expected to rise by 61% from $3,659 to $6,034 (Keehan et al., 2023).

Figure 1.1 shows the percentage of GDP spent on healthcare among the United States and 12 other OECD countries from 1980 to 2021. You

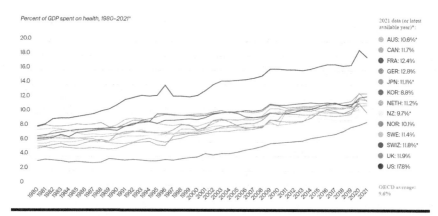

Figure 1.1 Percent of GDP Spent on Health 1980–2021

Source: Gunja, M. Z., Gumas, E. D., & Williams, R. D., II (January 22, 2023). U.S. health care from a global perspective, 2022: Accelerating spending, worsening outcomes. *Commonwealth Fund. https://doi.org/10.26099/8ejy-yc74*

can see from the top line of the graph that the United States has long been an outlier in this statistic.

1.3 U.S. Healthcare Spending as a Share of Total Spend

Perhaps more shocking than the percentage of GDP numbers is the sheer amount of money that the United States spends on healthcare. But, still, let's stick with GDP for a moment to get some perspective. According to The World Bank (2023), GDP in the United States was $25.5 trillion in 2022, while the total world GDP was $100.6 trillion, meaning that the United States accounts for a whopping 25% of the entire world's GDP.

So, now, let's look at how much actual money we spend on healthcare. Based on the latest numbers available for comparative purposes when we were writing this book, according to the World Health Organization, global health spending in 2019 was $8.5 trillion, with the United States accounting for 42% of that spending, or about $3.6 trillion. This is equivalent to the total healthcare expenditures of the 83 lowest spending countries combined. The 29 "high-income" countries (HIC-29) in the world accounted for approximately 76% of global healthcare spending, with the United States responsible for well over half of that amount (WHO, 2021).

These are good numbers to keep in mind as we go through this book. The United States generates 25% of the world's GDP, while, at the same time, it is spending 42% of what the entire world spends on healthcare. Let's also keep these numbers in mind: In September 2023, the United States had a population of 335 million, which was 4.1% of the total world population of 7.995 billion (U.S. Census Bureau, 2023).

1.4 Why Is Healthcare So Costly in America?

When people try to explain, or explain away, the extraordinary costs of healthcare in the United States, the easy answer seems to be how an OECD staff analysis in 2022 started its description of the problem:

> The United States is a rich country, so it is normal that it spends more on health. The richer a country is, the greater the resources it devotes to health care as citizens' demands for more care increases.
>
> **(Morgan et al., 2022)**

But that very true statement is immediately qualified with the next sentence: "However, even taking into account the overall wealth of the United States, its spending on health is comparatively high."

The authors, using more than a decade of OECD data, laid out this relationship between income and health spending. Using the examples of the lower income countries of the Slovak Republic and Hungary, they note that if per capita income is approximately $20,000, a country might be "expected" to spend around $2,000 per person on healthcare. Double that to $40,000 in per capita income, and the expected per capita spending might be threefold, or $6,000.

The authors note that this relationship may be a bit oversimplified, but it makes a convenient way to compare. They state that even though the United States has the highest level of wealth and household consumption, it is still far above what would be considered expected healthcare expenditures. They estimate that at its 2022 income level, the United States should be spending approximately $2,500 per capita less than it is spending, which would result in a savings of approximately $800 billion per year.

Considering, as we noted above, that the United States has nearly $5,000 per capita higher healthcare expenditures than the next-highest OECD member, Germany (also a very wealthy country), it seems like we have a lot of work to do in lowering costs.

The OECD analysis states that evidence suggests a major cause of high healthcare spending in the United States is the much higher prices of medical goods and services relative to other G7 countries. However, even considering those higher prices, the researchers note that it may also be true that a relatively high volume of healthcare-related goods and services (high utilization) is contributing to those spending levels.

1.5 What Does All of This Spending Mean for Quality Outcomes?

In 2021, the United States spent $4.3 trillion on healthcare (Martin et al., 2022). One would think that this level of spending would result in better health outcomes for the population. According to a Commonwealth Fund analysis of the 2022 OECD Health Statistics data on the 13 highest income OECD countries, this is not the case (Gunja et al., 2023). Among the researchers' findings in that analysis were the following:

- The United States has the highest rates of infant mortality and maternal mortality.
- The highest level of avoidable deaths per 100,000 population (336) occurs in the United States, which is well above all high-income OECD countries and the overall OECD average (225).
- Adults in the United States are the most likely to have multiple chronic conditions.
- The United States has the lowest rates of physician visits and practicing physicians.
- The United States had the highest rate of death because of COVID-19 from January 2020 to January 2023.
- Only Switzerland has a higher rate of hip replacements than the United States.

Speaking of high-end implantable medical devices (IMDs), as we covered in our first book, healthcare provider organizations in the United States pay far more for them than their counterparts in other countries, up to six times more in some cases (West & Georgulis, 2023). We also pointed out that part of those costs were due to revisions and replacements, which contribute to that high utilization level of medical goods and services that the OECD analysis touched upon in the previous section.

The bulleted list above shows statistics regarding how the United States compares against the 13 highest income OECD countries. In addition to the poor outcome data presented above, among all OECD countries, the United States ranks on the low end of outcomes in other key areas, including the following (Peter G. Peterson Foundation, 2023):

■ Infant mortality: Japan ranks best in this measure at 1.7 deaths per 1,000 live births, while Colombia is worst at 16.5. The United States stands at 5.4.

■ Unaddressed diabetes: Japan ranks best in this measure at 6.2 deaths per 100,00 population, while Turkey is worst at 32.5. The United States stands at 31.

■ Unaddressed asthma: Japan, again, is best in this measure at 0.5 deaths per 100,00 population, while Turkey is worst at 3.17. The United States stands at 1.3.

When it comes to life expectancy at birth among the 13 highest income countries, OECD 2021 data in Figure 1.2 again show the United States as an outlier (bottom line of the figure), and not in a good way, with U.S. life expectancy (77.0 years) three years lower than average of all 38 OECD countries (80.4 years) and below all of the 13 highest income OECD countries.

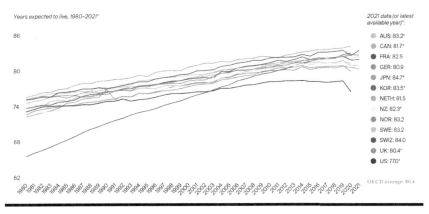

Figure 1.2 Years Expected to Live 1980–2021

Source: Gunja, M. Z., Gumas, E. D., & Williams, R. D., II (January 22, 2023). U.S. health care from a global perspective, 2022: Accelerating spending, worsening outcomes. Commonwealth Fund. https://doi.org/10.26099/8ejy-yc74

1.6 The Growing Cost Burden in Health Systems

Of all of the entities in the healthcare industry, it is health systems that are having perhaps the greatest difficulty controlling their cost structures. As the healthcare industry works to recover from the effects of the pandemic, health systems especially must find solutions for gaining that control.

According to a study from the American Hospital Association (AHA, 2023), more than half of U.S. hospitals ended 2022 operating with a financial loss. The report also cites data from the Medicare Inpatient Prospective Payment System (IPPS) showing that from 2019 through 2022, cumulative hospital expense growth was 17.5%, while, at the same time, Medicare IPPS reimbursement rose only 7.5%.

The AHA study points out that from 2019 through 2022, nonlabor costs—chiefly drugs, medical supplies, and equipment and purchased services expenses—rose 16.6%.

As we pointed out in our first book, pharmaceutical and medical device manufacturing sectors are doing relatively well because of their ability to control their costs and their robust internal alignment.

To stay solvent, health systems are raising prices. These costs trickle (or flood) down to the insurers, who are also doing well. Unfortunately, in the process, skyrocketing provider health system costs are passed on to employers and patients in increased premiums and deductibles, raising the cost of doing business across a wide range of industries and affecting their workforce and growth considerations.

The authors of the AHA study concluded, "The combination of the impacts on hospitals of the ending public health emergency as well as continued expense growth has created an uncertain future for hospitals and health systems."

Two healthcare industry segments of suppliers consistently represent notoriously high costs to U.S. hospitals and healthcare systems relative to those of other countries—the IMD and pharmaceutical industries. Both have enjoyed strong growth over the past few decades and will continue that growth, according to recent forecasts.

Two major market research firms recently made comparable projections about the phenomenal growth the global IMD market will experience in the coming decade. In 2022, market research and consulting firm Prophecy Market Insights estimated that the IMD market accounted for $98.6 billion in value in 2022 and through 2032 is expected to grow at a compound annual growth rate (CAGR) of 7.2%, reaching $166.3 billion valuation by the end of 2032. Verified Market Research in 2023 valued the 2022 IMD market at $101.8 billion and forecasted it would grow to

$158.4 billion in 2030, at a CAGR of 6.52% (Prophecy Market Insights, 2022; Verified Market Research, 2023).

In pharmaceuticals, which is a much larger healthcare segment, growth is also projected to be robust.

Statista Market Insights, a leading provider of market and consumer data, projects that revenue in the global pharmaceuticals market will reach $1.16 trillion in 2023 and show an annual CAGR from 2023 through 2027 of 5.39%, rising to a market volume of $1.435 trillion. The report notes that a great share of that revenue—$624.1 billion—will be generated in the United States (Statista, 2023).

We point out the growth in these two supplier segments not to imply that there is anything wrong with IMD manufacturers or pharmaceutical companies—or any company for that matter—making a profit and having robust industries. We are businesspeople, and we believe in healthy markets. One desired outcome would be healthy competition on those two facets of value: quality and cost. Cost equity is a problem that must be addressed as well, as can be seen in the statistics that have been presented in this chapter. Competition doesn't exist in a world dominated by oligopoly spending and where spend equity is nonexistent. We will detail these challenges and some proposed solutions starting in Chapter 4, where we introduce the Lacuna Triangle.

Our concern is that the lacunas, or gaps, that have inhibited our hospital and health system supply chains' ability to do effective strategic sourcing have been instrumental in creating oligopolies, irrational markets, and irrational pricing throughout the U.S. healthcare system.

We believe the solution to these overarching challenges in healthcare of quality and cost need to start on the ground floor with the supply chains in each of our provider health system organizations, especially those that have the demonstrated ability to commit the kind of volume that makes suppliers sit up and take notice. To start getting some rationality back into health system markets, we recommend starting with the supply chain.

1.7 The Importance of the Supply Chain in Healthcare

When we think of supply chain in manufacturing, we consider what it takes to put together a product for a consumer. The product can range in complexity from an automobile to a frozen burrito bowl to a bar of soap. In manufacturing, the supply chain's goal might also be to put together a product that supplies a service industry that serves a consumer. Think aircraft manufacturer → airline → traveler.

In healthcare, we are in a unique service industry where the supply chain's goal is to provide the enterprise with a vast array of goods and services that enable the workers to do their jobs in serving the end customer. In essence, without the supply chain in healthcare, there are no jobs because there is no capacity to provide services.

Traditionally in healthcare, the analysis of how to cut costs has focused on billing and services. As we noted earlier in this chapter, administrative costs are extraordinarily high in American healthcare relative to other wealthy countries, so that is a good place to start.

We mentioned that efforts are under way in response to the failures during the pandemic, and parts of those efforts are on the right track in theory, including getting the end of the supply chain back closer to our shores and nurturing the supplier market.

But we need to dig much deeper into the core issues, starting with the supply chain operations within hospitals and health systems and their relationship with suppliers and their effect on the market.

1.8 Moving on to a Model for Strategic Sourcing

In this chapter we have laid out some of the challenges in U.S. healthcare in costs and healthcare outcomes in which the current healthcare supply chain operates. We have also touched on an overall solution that starts with effective strategic sourcing that is run within the supply chain management department. We have stated that we are not there yet in the healthcare industry though many health systems may think they are doing effective strategic sourcing.

In the next chapter we explain what strategic sourcing is, its evolution, examples of organizations who have found success with it, and what the model looks like, including the scope of responsibilities for high-performing strategic sourcing operations within a healthcare organization's supply chain management system.

References

American Hospital Association. (2023). *The financial stability of America's hospitals and health systems is at risk as the costs of caring continue to rise.* www.aha.org/ system/files/media/file/2023/04/Cost-of-Caring-2023-The-Financial-Stability-of-Americas-Hospitals-and-Health-Systems-Is-at-Risk.pdf

Gartner. (July 12, 2023). *The Gartner supply chain top 25 for 2023.* www.gartner.com/en/supply-chain/research/supply-chain-top-25

Gunja, M. Z., Gumas, E. D., & Williams, R. D., II (January 22, 2023). *U.S. health care from a global perspective, 2022: Accelerating spending, worsening outcomes.* Commonwealth Fund. https://doi.org/10.26099/8ejy-yc74

Keehan, S. P., Fiore, J. A., Poisel, J. A., Cuckler, G. A., Sisko, A. M., Smith, S. D., Jackson, A. J., & Rennie, K. E. (June 14, 2023). National health expenditure projections, 2022–31: Growth to stabilize once the COVID-19 public health emergency ends. *Health Affairs.* www.healthaffairs.org/doi/10.1377/hlthaff.2023.00403

Martin, A. B., Hartman, M., Benson, J., Catlin, A., & The National Health Expenditure Accounts Team. (December 14, 2022). National health care spending in 2021: Decline in federal spending outweighs greater use of health care. *Health Affairs,* 42(1). https://doi.org/10.1377/hlthaff.2022.01397

Morgan, D., Lorenzoni, L., Colombo, F., Scarpetta, S., & Pearson, M. (September 2022). *Understanding differences in health expenditure between the United States and OECD countries.* Organisation for Economic Co-Operation and Development (OECD). www.oecd.org/health/Health-expenditure-differences-USA-OECD-countries-Brief-July-2022.pdf

Organisation for Economic Co-Operation and Development (OECD). (2020). *2020 health statistics.* Online Database. https://stats.oecd.org

Peter G. Peterson Foundation. (2023). *How does the U.S. healthcare system compare to other countries?* www.pgpf.org/blog/2022/07/how-does-the-us-healthcare-system-compare-to-other-countries

Prophecy Market Insights. (December 2022). *Implantable medical devices market—trends, analysis, and forecast till 2032.* www.prophecymarketinsights.com/market_insight/Implantable-Medical-Devices-Market-5026

Statista. (2023). *Statista health market outlook: Pharmaceuticals—market data analysis and forecasts.* www.statista.com/outlook/hmo/pharmaceuticals/worldwide

Teisberg, E., Wallace, S., & O'Hara, S. (2020). Defining and implementing value-based health care: A strategic framework. *Academic Medicine,* 95(5), 682–685. www.ncbi.nlm.nih.gov/pmc/articles/PMC7185050/

U.S. Census Bureau. (2023). *U.S. and world population clock.* Retrieved September 3, 2023, from www.census.gov/popclock/world

Verified Market Research. (June 2023). *Implantable medical devices market size and forecast.* www.verifiedmarketresearch.com/product/implantable-medical-devices-market/

West, M. C., & Georgulis, M. (2023). *Implantable medical devices and healthcare affordability: Exposing the spiderweb.* Routledge Taylor & Francis Group.

The World Bank. (2023). *GDP (current U.S. $).* https://data.worldbank.org/indicator/NY.GDP.MKTP.CD

World Health Organization (WHO). (2021). *Global expenditure on health: Public spending on the rise?* www.who.int/publications/i/item/9789240041219

Chapter 2

What is Strategic Sourcing?

"If you can't describe what you are doing as a process, you don't know what you're doing."

– W. Edwards Deming

In this chapter we will present the process of strategic sourcing not from the current healthcare perspective, but from the perspective of a non-healthcare industry. The practices, procedures, process, and outcomes warrant a comparison to appreciate healthcare's conundrum.

If you ask people the question, "Where would you go to get the best price for gas?" they would probably answer something like this: "On the intersection where there's a gas station on all four corners." Makes sense. At intersections like these, the gas station proprietors are often in heated competition to have the lowest price, or at least the perception of the best quality for a fairly low price.

So, it stands to reason if you were the leader of a major corporate office or a major health system and you wanted all your employees to get the best price for gas for official use with the company gas card you would send them to that intersection.

In the absence of a high-performing strategic sourcing model, this may seem like a great idea. So, let's look at the gas station example for a moment through the lens of a best-in-class, mature strategic sourcing model.

 DOI: 10.4324/9781003495291-3

As a simple illustration, consider a strategy instead in which you are a corporation's strategic sourcing executive, and you approach the four gas station proprietors on this corner and propose that every one of your organization's employees buys gas only from one station. And, for example, from the gas station proprietor's perspective this would represent 30% of their sales volume and if they agree they will know that 30% of their sales volume will be guaranteed from this one source. In return, you negotiate that your employees have their own dedicated gas station pumps. Also, instead of giving them Regular (87 octane) gas, they get Mid-grade (89 octane) gas, and they get it at 10 cents less per gallon than the lowest current price on the street corner.

In addition, you also want them to provide an attendant who pumps the gas for your employees, so the employees that are getting gas filled don't have to get out of their vehicles. An advantage to the gas station would be customer cycle time.

Also, instead of having your employees hand the attendant a credit card for a transaction every time your employees buy gas, you want the attendant to scan the employee's badge and their license plate and then once a month send summary billing. This is an efficiency benefit that accounts payable has been seeking support on. With that billing process, we could also receive a detailed report of company purchases. This should cut down on fraud, because we will put a barcode on the car to ensure they're not putting gas in their personal vehicles.

Finally, we periodically receive copies of their quality control process and gas testing data and results to ensure the fuel will not damage company vehicles.

So, how might this serve the interest of the gas station proprietor, in exchange for giving the lowest price? First, they are guaranteed 30% of their sales volume, so that means they could approach their distributors for additional price concessions and obtain more favorable loan rates and payment terms with their creditors. Summary billing allows the station proprietor to avoid credit card transaction fees, which are usually about 3% of the transaction amount. If employees have a positive experience at the gas station, they will likely use it for their personal needs. Also, when this model works and becomes profitable for the gas station proprietor, then they could go to other corporate headquarters and offer the same model to them, generating a higher percentage of sales volume commitment for themselves.

This example speaks to a collaborative approach to key suppliers and gets us much closer to what an effective corporate chief supply chain officer would expect from strategic sourcing leaders.

Originally, we wanted our employees to buy gas at a four-way inter-section that had many gas stations and buy the lowest posted rate. But the idea of going to that intersection and finding which of the four gas stations has the lowest price and then going there with your gas card to buy gas is a purely transactional exercise. The strategic sourcing execu-tive, on the other hand, wants to build the best solution from a quality, financial, and operational perspective that benefits both parties—the cor-poration and the selected gas station/supplier.

Again, this example represents what is at the "core" of strategic sourc-ing. It also has the element of understanding each other's "interests" and working to satisfy those through negotiations and an agreement that benefits both parties. The negotiation process in strategic sourcing is not an effort of one party to get a leg up on the other, but an effort for each party to find the benefits of an agreement.

To understand why the gas station example works, it is important to appreciate the interests of the supplier. A supplier's goal is to get as close as possible to having 100% sold product coming off of the production line at all times. In this example, it was a commitment of 30% of the supplier's sales volume that they knew would be sold coming off the line. Even though this is not a true production line, it is the same concept.

So, what does volume commitment mean? As a health system or other corporate entity, if you have scale, it means being able to commit that volume, and having a supplier know over an agreement period of two to five years exactly how much of their product coming off the production line is already sold. This seriously reduces their cost of sales, which factors in expense reduction.

So, another key issue to consider in this equation is mutual interest. In the gas station scenario, we wanted to get gas at a favorable price, and we wanted our employees to efficiently select, acquire, and pay for the product. The interest of the gas station proprietor is committed volume, and wanting committed revenue in a model that they could scale to other customers if it worked. So, in this simple example, there was mutual inter-est in working together.

This gas station example is based on a discussion one of the authors had with a healthcare clinical leader about 15 years ago to explain the dif-ferences between transactional purchasing and strategic sourcing. While the example is dated, the illustration created a willingness on the part of the clinical leader to pilot strategic sourcing efforts that became standard practice at Cleveland Clinic.

Strategic sourcing is integral to our supply chain management efforts in healthcare, but it goes far beyond the traditional concepts of purchasing and fulfillment. Strategic sourcing is fluid—continually evaluating and reevaluating quality, financial, operational, and organizational needs—and its success requires intensive alignment throughout the enterprise.

2.1 The Evolution of Strategic Sourcing

Strategic sourcing is a mature concept in many industries. It had its beginnings in the late 1980s through the 1990s. It is no coincidence that this period also saw the explosion in information technology and the internet as well as new global supply sources.

Advances in information and internet technology helped organizations begin to more effectively collect and analyze data not only internally on their own operations and finances related to them but also externally on potential suppliers of products and services needed to run operations.

Concurrently, there was significant growth of global supply opportunities, especially in Asia, eastern Europe, and even in neighboring countries such as Mexico. Initiatives such as the North American Free Trade Agreement (NAFTA) accelerated new supplier options that provided new challenges in evaluating, selecting, and managing suppliers that are logistically further away and culturally different.

The strategic sourcing model has been used successfully for decades. The following list of some of the biggest names who are recognized for employing strategic sourcing (Ozsevim, 2023) demonstrates the wide range of industries it is applied in:

- Walmart
- General Electric
- Nestlé
- Amazon
- Johnson & Johnson
- Apple Inc.
- Proctor & Gamble
- BMW Group
- Coca-Cola
- Toyota.

While not exhaustive, in this list, we have automobile manufacturers and distributors, brick-and-mortar and online retailers, a personal care and hygiene consumer goods giant, the leading computer and consumer electronics company, the world's largest diversified food and beverages company, and a manufacturer of healthcare products for consumer, pharmaceutical, and medical devices markets. That last-mentioned type of manufacturer, which is Johnson & Johnson, is obviously one of the types of suppliers we will be addressing throughout this book, as is General Electric, and not only its GE Healthcare division.

Actually, every company on this list is a potential supplier for us in healthcare, as we also look beyond the more clinically oriented products one would expect in the healthcare supply chain. In hospitals and health systems, we also need computers, vehicles, generators, food, and much more.

The point of this list is simple: If all of these industry giants are committed to a robust strategic sourcing process in their supply chain and procurement management operations, what has stunted the process in healthcare? That is a question for a later chapter. For now, we will continue with what strategic sourcing overall looks like.

2.2 The Strategic Part of Strategic Sourcing

The strategic sourcing process has many variations but is commonly broken into seven steps widely popularized by consulting firm A. T. Kearney (now called Kearney) beginning in the early 2000s. These steps are paraphrased from our perspective below:

1. Analyze your product categories, identifying the spending patterns and volumes for outside products and services. Conduct a needs analysis among internal customers and departments.
2. Develop your market approach and create a sourcing strategy based on quality, financial, and operational considerations.
3. After creating supplier selection criteria based on internal customer needs, study the supplier market, and create a portfolio of suitable suppliers.
4. Develop criteria for your requests for proposals (RFP), and create customized RFP templates weighted with your criteria.
5. Conduct the RFP process, and negotiate with selected suppliers, with an eye toward driving preferable supplier behaviors.
6. Transition suppliers into your strategic sourcing processes. Develop and implement an onboarding process for new vendors and suppliers.
7. Track performance of your strategic sourcing process, and use intensive analytics to refine your sourcing plan and strengthen alignment throughout the process.

2.3 Enterprise Alignment: The Role of Leadership in Strategic Sourcing

As we presented in our first book, *Implantable Medical Devices and Healthcare Affordability: Exposing the Spiderweb*, enterprise alignment is key to success in supply chain management (SCM). Alignment in the sense we are describing here goes far beyond merely having everyone's agreement that the strategic sourcing process is the right thing to do in the organization. The entire enterprise is aligned by budgets, goals, personal and departmental performance expectations, and even bonuses. Strategic sourcing is aligned into the culture of the organization and its strategic imperatives.

To drive this alignment through the organization and ultimately downstream to the internal customers, most organizations that do strategic sourcing well have invested in and accepted a C-suite-level executive onboard with the title of Chief Supply Chain Officer (CSCO) or Chief Procurement Officer (CPO) or more recently some even with the title, Chief Sourcing Officer (CSO). We prefer CSCO for the purposes of this book, even though our main subject is strategic sourcing. Whatever their title, having this person at the highest level of the organization demonstrates the seriousness the organization attaches to robust alignment around SCM. Remember, in many organizations the supply chain is frequently one of the top two biggest expenses, so it is so much more than a simple order-processing exercise, as it is commonly seen in organizations that lack strategy and alignment around sourcing.

So, driving that alignment throughout the organization requires leadership, influence, and relationship skills that are rewarded with C-suite participation. The CSCOs must first utilize those skills to educate, influence, and align their peers around a best-in-class strategic sourcing process addressing both the clinical and nonclinical needs of the enterprise. The CSCO leads a team that goes far beyond their direct reports to people inside the enterprise's various departments or divisions with deep knowledge of their own quality, financial, and operational needs. The CSCO is pivotal to developing and maintaining the relationships that drive alignment around strategic sourcing with the internal customers of the enterprise.

Then, there is the external environment, where the CSCO becomes the public face of the organization's commitment to quality, value, relationships, and process that deliver credibility. This is where the CSCO and their team project the organization's seriousness about alignment around true strategic sourcing to the outside world, especially for suppliers.

Internal customers learn to view the CSCO and their team as strategic partners. External individuals and entities, such as suppliers, view the CSCO and their team members as the faces of the organization. And in those faces they see the rigorous strategic sourcing commitment that the enterprise communicates and aligns around. This also delivers a level of sophistication that this team brings to negotiations. The CSCO has credibility as the decision authority, so supplier games such as going around the supply chain to gain influence with internal stakeholders that might work with some organizations are going to be difficult with this one. This is why developing a supplier collaborative approach and integrating suppliers into your process are key components of strategic sourcing.

2.4 Seeking Solutions: The Strategic Sourcing Department

The role of the strategic sourcing department—if that is what you choose to call your group—is finding the optimal solution to meet the enterprise's needs from quality, financial, and operational perspectives. In essence, the department is purchasing all the goods and services that the organization has decided not to produce or provide themselves. This could be a wide range of items that might include outsourcing seats in the case of an aircraft manufacturer, or pill containers for a pharmaceutical company, or heart valves for a hospital, or for all types of organizations it might be janitorial or security services.

So, everything that an organization decides not to make or do themselves is acquired through the strategic sourcing process to support the enterprise. And when we say supporting the enterprise, it means the whole enterprise. When many people think about supply chain management in the manufacturing world, they envision end-to-end sourcing—from raw materials to finished goods. However, in the case of automotive or aircraft manufacturers, for example, SCM goes far beyond the assembly line for the products they produce. They also need furniture, computers, office supplies, food services, office cleaning, security, marketing services, and more for their employees.

The strategic sourcing group is tasked with gaining an understanding of the products or services as well as the operational and administrative requirements associated with buying those goods or services. To do this, they must answer questions like the following:

■ Does it need to meet certain quality standards?
■ Must it be delivered on a certain day or with certain lead times?
■ Are there specific inventory levels that need to be maintained?
■ Is specific administrative paperwork needed from a quality perspective?
■ Does the product need to be in a climate-controlled environment?

Strategic sourcing is being able to find that optimal solution in the market to fill a specific organizational need. This requires a detailed process that starts by working with all internal customers and their departments.

Looking outside of the organization, strategic sourcing entails performing research, scouring the market for essential as well as efficient solutions, and working with key suppliers to determine the best solution for meeting all the requirements of internal stakeholders. Suppliers often have relationships within an enterprise with the same key internal stakeholders as strategic sourcing professionals. In healthcare, this might be physicians; in the aircraft industry, it may be with machinists and engineers; in construction, it might be with company architects. Recognizing this fact as well as keeping that thought in front of mind will be extremely beneficial.

Strategic sourcing includes how the payment and transaction processes will be conducted among your organization and all the various suppliers, and additionally, how a supplier conversion process may be successfully implemented.

Let's consider the sourcing of packaging materials for products. When packaging is being sourced, considerable research is required. We may know of three or four manufacturers of packaging. We mine our data on packaging and begin to break down the cost structure of products acquired over the prior 12 months and match that with which products they have to offer. We should be working with our internal customers and the suppliers to gain an understanding of the known quality indicators and what research requirements have been fulfilled on these products. This is all done in the interest of building a sourcing plan that all stakeholders can align with.

From the research performed, we may determine that we can standardize and rationalize both products and suppliers from the original four suppliers in this example down to two. Once this is accomplished, we can begin working on agreement terms and conditions with prospective suppliers, laying out the type of contract desired, including, but certainly not limited to, the quality, delivery, conversion, and billing process expectations.

2.5 How the Strategic Sourcing Group Works

A high-performing, top-tier strategic sourcing function has dedicated and committed resources. Usually, there is a strategic sourcing executive who leads a team within the supply chain management department. Also, within the department are strategic sourcing directors, managers, and specialists/analysts who lead teams that focus on specified categories of goods and services on behalf of the enterprise. Again, these roles are filled by individuals who represent both technical and nontechnical abilities and inputs who would be considered subject matter experts (SMEs). The teams might divide the work up among the following category examples:

- Teams would manage packaging products, electronic components, and engine parts.
- Others could manage food services, janitorial, parking, and security.
- Others might handle office supplies and facilities-related procurement or capital equipment.

To effectively source goods and services for their internal customers, strategic sourcing professionals must build a series of formal and informal internal relationships, which include legal, risk management, accounting, quality, operations, IT/security, treasury, and more. Sometimes these resources are "dotted line" relationships (like having a person in the legal department that reviews supplier contracts) or a funded headcount within the supply chain department (like a supplier development engineer that audits high-risk suppliers to ensure source of supply).

Back to the "strategic" nature of strategic sourcing for a moment. In this sense, the heart and vascular products leader of the strategic sourcing team should have a seat at the table in the cardiology-related meetings. This person should be integrated into cardiology issues, such as budgets, where the budget discussions are held for the purpose of understanding goods and services that are "budget approved" for a strategic sourcing process and for the department's core business.

The heart and vascular products leader should be embedded with the appropriate cardiology-related departments, units, or specialty clinics and hospitals, learning about issues, such as new and developing technologies, which products might be experiencing quality issues, which suppliers are delivering the best services and new technology, and other important knowledge that aligns with finding the best solution from quality, operational, and clinical perspectives. This creates credibility that strategic sourcing represents the needs of the cardiology entity. The insight they gain allows them to fully align with and support the entity.

This intimate relationship provides the platform for collaboration that is necessary to conduct high-performing strategic sourcing. The strategic sourcing leader helps design and leads the negotiations, the contracting, and all the activities of the category leaders, and there is complete alignment and intensive collaboration around developing these outcomes.

The scope of responsibilities for a high-performing strategic sourcing department within a supply chain operation is wide-ranging. It includes, but is not limited to, the following:

- Monitoring, documenting, and informing on industry market trends and variation
- Managing relationships with and among suppliers and internal customers
- Understanding and meeting internal customer needs as they evolve
- Defining and managing hundreds of product categories
- Creating, managing, and overseeing thousands of supplier contracts
- Ensuring that strategically sourced products and services exceed expectations
- Contributing to having the right products at the right place at the right time with the utmost efficiency.

High-performing strategic sourcing departments pull all of these tremendous responsibilities together by utilizing documented, well-defined, and aligned category strategies within their enterprise. Rather than narrowly prioritizing the focus on creating and managing supplier contracts, successful strategic sourcing puts a priority on managing categories and relationships through an aligned, "living," end-to-end process that is continuously evaluated and improved.

In strategic sourcing, resources are dedicated to a structured process for developing and implementing aligned solutions that, again, best meet the quality, financial and operational, needs of the organization. This is accomplished through the lens of multiple purchase categories as mentioned above.

2.6 The "Relationship" Aspect of Category Strategies in Strategic Sourcing

Consider the "relationships" aspect as these category strategy documents are developed and formally agreed upon between the strategic sourcing category leader and a departmental team of internal customers whose functions rely on fulfillment of specific collections of product and service categories.

Implementing strategic sourcing using category strategies helps SCM professionals become organized and synchronized with internal customers. It also demonstrates to C-suite leadership that SCM is using a rigorous process for considering all variables and explaining the logic for strategic decisions and supplier performance. Additionally, having defined category strategies with consolidated information makes onboarding new SCM professionals into a department or into another category much more efficient.

Category strategies also help establish and develop the organization's culture. The collaborative effort of developing and managing these lasting and evolving documents requires trusting, engaged relationships among internal customers. Through the process, strategic sourcing staff members become integral to internal customer meetings as a voice in helping guide departments through planning for their current and future operational challenges. They also become integral to the internal annual budgeting processes, helping departments anticipate changes in volumes, capital needs, and the necessary mix of products.

On the supplier relationship side, the enterprise realizes the benefits of being an important and key customer. In this collaborative environment created by category strategies, suppliers begin to benefit from higher levels of engagement, consistency of message, and greater commitment from the enterprise. All of these lend to the important "credibility" requirement suppliers look for when calculating exposure on delivered value in an agreement.

2.7 The Responsibility of Strategic Sourcing

Strategic sourcing experts must be stewards of building markets that are rational and balanced, which means that healthy competition thrives, and the availability of goods and services remains robust. This requires understanding the consequences of committed strategic sourcing efforts that may shrink or expand the supplier base. If we remember our gas station example, it would mean making certain that our strategy of purchasing from only one gas station would not jeopardize future product availability within a competitive market.

As we alluded to in the first paragraph of this chapter, healthcare providers and GPOs handle strategic sourcing in a very different manner than described in this chapter. Their sourcing lacks the strategic component, and it is conducted in the midst of highly irrational and unbalanced markets. In Chapter 3, we detail the state of "strategic" sourcing in healthcare today and how it results in that irrationality and imbalance.

Reference

Ozsevim, I. (2023). Top 10 examples of strategic sourcing. *Procurement.* https://procurementmag.com/articles/top-10-examples-of-strategic-sourcing

Chapter 3

"Strategic Sourcing" in Healthcare Today

3.1 Healthcare's Use of "Strategic Sourcing"

Before we explain where strategic sourcing is today in healthcare, we would like to take you back to the beginning of the 2010s and an organization we created, then called SharedClarity. SharedClarity was a dual-purpose organization: It was a clinical organization designed to conduct studies on medical devices and determine best performance based on patient outcomes after implantation, and it was a strategic sourcing organization aggregating membership volume and going to market for a differentiated value.

We were seen as an aggregator—defined overall as an organization that aggregates the volume of a group of hospitals and health systems into a membership arrangement whose goals are to get them a better price on goods and services. By that broad definition, our organization could have been lumped in with the GPOs of the day.

SharedClarity, however, had a much different way of going about the aggregation business, focusing on specific categories of products, rather than the full gamut of what a health system or hospital procures. The name came from the concept that we were providing shared clarity and transparency for our members into the true evidence-based performance and costs of the implantable medical device categories in which we were working. SharedClarity was a joint venture of several large health systems

 DOI: 10.4324/9781003495291-4

and one of the largest commercial payers in the country. Without getting into too much of the detail of the organization, for the purposes of this chapter, we will present a scenario of how SharedClarity went about its sourcing process.

First, our EVA process was designed to gain intelligence on how implantable medical devices (IMD) performed, then gain clinical consensus, which allowed the strategic sourcing process to consolidate, standardize, and rationalize suppliers of IMDs, with a sharp focus on improving knowledge about IMD performance and affordability. We will detail value analysis later in this chapter and in Chapter 5. For now, it is important to note that the two main areas of emphasis in our EVA process—performance and affordability—are not so coincidentally the two prominent areas of focus in what we today call value-based care—quality health outcomes for patients at the lowest cost.

Notice we don't say lowest *price* because the price of something is simply a price. The ultimate *value* of something is a wholly different animal. Determining the value of a device versus what its price is requires research, and that means data.

3.2 The Value of Data in Determining Real Costs

Having both a large payer and large health systems in the SharedClarity venture was essential to such an ambitious strategic sourcing enterprise. The health systems have electronic health record (EHR) data from patients, while the large commercial payer has medical claims data that can often close the loop on both the outcomes and costs experienced by the patient.

For example, a hospital discharges a patient after a knee implant procedure that seems to have gone well. A month or so later the implant recipient is experiencing a decrease in joint function, stiffness, swelling, and significant pain. An examination reveals that a revision is required, but the patient seeks care with a different orthopedic surgeon and hospital from where the first procedure was done.

This could happen for many reasons. For example, the patient moved to a different geographical area, or "in plan" physicians changed, which precluded the same physician from being used. Maybe the original physician retired or moved the practice to a different town. Then, there are those patients who after having an implant go bad don't have the confidence that returning to the same hospital or physician will produce a better outcome.

So, the first hospital/provider will have one group of costs for that patient but not necessarily accurate outcome information. The second hospital/provider will have a second set of costs for that patient and perhaps an accurate outcome. If we were the first surgeon/hospital combination, we would probably report that the patient had a good outcome and relatively low costs. But looking in from the outside, one would not understand the complications, the revision, the costs incurred, and what the ultimate cost was. They also wouldn't know if the problem was a defective implant from the supplier or errors on the surgical or hospital side.

This is where having the major payer's data can come in handy, because their claims data can close the loop on the entire story for that implant patient. Two minimum sets of data must be available for this determination to occur, and SharedClarity had access to them. First, we must know what manufacturer's product was implanted in all cases, and second, we must be able to follow the patient through the care continuum.

SharedClarity's value analysis and strategic sourcing structure closely followed what we explained in Chapter 2 that is done in other industries. It was an EVA process. In collaboration with SharedClarity, member health system leaders formed a clinical effectiveness committee for IMDs that had physician-led subcommittees for different categories, such as cardiology and orthopedics. The process allowed input about IMD performance and affordability to flow up from *all* of the physician specialists throughout the health systems who used the IMDs being selected in the agreements and through to a physician-led selection committee.

Through a combination of studying existing literature, quality, and safety information on the products, outcomes data from the health systems, and medical claims data from the payer, they were able to come to consensus on device performance and affordability. Armed with this information from this rigorous physician-led consolidation and rationalization process, SharedClarity then conducted sourcing and negotiations for agreements with suppliers that were built on the foundation of volume commitment.

Having physician consensus on device specifications and performance in the category prior to conducting a strategic sourcing event allowed the sourcing event to focus on a result of reducing the quantity of suppliers to be selected and used in the member health systems. The result was 30–50% price reductions for the health systems on the IMDs under these new contracts as compared to the previous agreements. Note that the SharedClarity member "previous agreements" comparisons in these instances were prices compared against their GPO price files in place at the time we validated savings. Physicians also then knew they were using devices that performed to the high-quality standards they demanded.

The reason this worked, and that leadership, physicians, supply chain staff, and suppliers all got onboard, was that everyone knew we had full commitment and alignment in the process, and that is what the rest of this chapter is about.

3.3 A Divergent View of Strategic Sourcing

High-performing strategic sourcing—the likes of which we detailed in Chapter 2—is not evident for the most part in the U.S. healthcare supply chain, neither in provider health systems, nor in GPOs. In most provider health systems today, strategic sourcing has simply become an exercise in creating contracts or modifying GPO contracts with those who already have manufactured products or a defined set of service offerings in their pipeline and then delivering those products and services to provider organizations for use by physicians, nurses, and other service providers in the facilities for the benefit of their patients. Frequently, little if any independent strategies are applied by health systems beyond the GPO supplier contract.

So, what is the basic difference when considering strategic sourcing in other industries as presented earlier? First, in other industries, the process includes activities such as, but is not limited to, the following:

- Supplier capability audits
- Demand forecasting
- Hedging high-cost raw materials
- Developing and encouraging new market entrants.

Other industries also often envision a manufacturing line where all these activities come together. In healthcare, because we source finished goods, we do not have a need to understand, nor does it seem that many leaders have a comprehensive understanding that, these process differences exist between industry and healthcare.

Another glaring difference between other industries and healthcare is that the providers, supply chain executives, and health systems rely on GPOs to do most of what they designate as strategic sourcing. GPOs dominate healthcare but have a limited presence or no presence in other industries. Some in healthcare argue that this is because the goods and services sourced in their industry are so numerous and wide ranging. However, there are many industries in the country in which the supply chain is just as, or much more, complex and their requirements are more precise and delicate than in healthcare. It makes sense that sourcing finished goods lends itself to an aggregation process more so than sourcing raw materials for production lines in many manufacturing industries.

The widespread belief that healthcare practices effective strategic sourcing is a misnomer. Generally speaking, healthcare organizational leaders in the United States believe that in relying on the GPO, they are participating in the process of strategic sourcing—it is just that the GPO is taking care of all those details we presented in Chapter 2. And the GPOs will insist that the confidence of those healthcare organizational leaders in that belief is well founded. Aggregating volume has resulted in an aggregation process that presumes one size fits all, and one result satisfies all. "Well-founded" may be the deceptive despair keeping them members of GPOs, given the fallacy that the safe harbor they operate under delivers value.

The truth is, GPOs are doing very little of what is considered strategic sourcing in other industries or in the healthcare systems of other countries that do not rely on GPOs. When U.S. healthcare organizations rely on GPOs for their strategic sourcing processes, they are merely selecting products and services from the suppliers and contracts that GPOs negotiate. As a side note, many physicians, nurses, and other end users of these GPO contract decisions and product selections are, by design, left out of the process.

In essence, hospitals and health systems are forfeiting the power they hold in their ability to commit volume for the financial benefit of other organizations, rather than for the benefit of their own enterprises.

The following is an explanation of what this process looks like. We will use pacemakers and defibrillators as an example of a product category in this "strategic sourcing" process.

3.4 How "Strategic Sourcing" Is Done in Healthcare Today

GPOs generally take about 12 months sourcing and negotiating a contract for a category, such as pacemakers and defibrillators. Based on how their health system member committees guide them, a GPO will create contracts with three or four of the major full line suppliers for those pacemakers and defibrillators that sometimes includes a "carve-out" for partial line suppliers. Most of the GPO agreement awards go to the major full line manufacturers in this category, such as Medtronic, Abbott, or Boston Scientific for example, versus manufacturers that only offer partial product lines.

Partial product line suppliers, for example, might include Oscor, Inc., which is a custom manufacturer of medical devices for cardiac and noncardiac applications, and Osypka Medtech Inc., a manufacturer of medical devices and equipment with electrophysiological, cardiac, and diagnostic applications whose products include catheters, leads, and pacemakers (Thomasnet, 2023).

Partial line suppliers may be awarded an agreement, but many times their award is limited to a small percentage of the total volume (such as 15% to 20%) as a "carve-out," but not a guarantee of business sales. Neither "full line" nor "partial line" speaks to quality of the products being manufactured, only to the extent of a manufacturer's offering.

Practically speaking, even with an award, the partial line suppliers have difficulty gaining market share because the full line suppliers will "bundle" their full line when they create their pricing tiers such that it could become cost-prohibitive to not select the full line of that manufacturer's offering. Picking and choosing a partial line supplier's products, even with the discounts they may offer, could not allow a health system to meet the volume requirements for a better priced tier of a full line supplier, significantly raising their cost in this category.

Vetting these IMDs is accomplished through the GPO member committees. These committees are generally comprised of clinical nurses, and on some committees, there will be a physician or two. The committee composition is usually a representation of 15 to 20 or more, depending on the GPO, of the largest member health systems. GPOs pull clinical nurses and physicians from this limited subset of their member health systems to represent the entire membership, and their input is used to make product and supplier selections. The selections these committees make don't necessarily get communicated to "all" member health systems until after selections have been made and agreements signed, if then.

3.5 "All-Play" Agreements versus Effective Strategic Sourcing

It is impossible to consolidate and rationalize at the GPO level. This would require thousands of hospitals and health systems with individual P&Ls located in diverse geographies with differing patient needs as a result of regional and multicultural differences, and tens of thousands of product end user physicians and nurses, and their C-suites to be aligned around the financial, operational, and clinical needs of their collective enterprise. Therefore, committee product and supplier selections for agreement awards are seldom the result of a process seeking to consolidate and rationalize products or suppliers. In fact, at times, they will expand the product selection and/or suppliers where possible. A GPO's sourcing process will generally result in what many term an "all-play" agreement. In these agreements most, if not all, suppliers in a particular category are awarded an agreement.

All-play agreements are reconciled at the health system level by offering numerous price tier levels from which any member health system can choose. In some instances there can be 30 or more tier levels within an agreement. This structure simply creates an environment where the price that a health system can select within the GPO agreements is often significantly higher than what they might be able to negotiate on their own, without a GPO agreement.

All-play agreements by design are not the result of a legitimate strategic sourcing process that values suppliers competing for business. As we presented in the previous chapter and in the introduction of SharedClarity above, strategic sourcing processes involve researching products and their manufacturers, aligning internal customers, C-suites, and suppliers, and then consolidating and rationalizing the number of suppliers down from five or six to two, or perhaps even one, based on aligned and accepted quality and value standards, and the needs of the enterprise. Such a process will eliminate the need for the multiple-tiered pricing schemes compelled in the GPO model of sourcing.

To further illustrate the concept of "tiered pricing," the following explanation may be helpful. Many tiers are often offered by suppliers in GPO agreements. Each supplier establishes their individual tiers and pricing, and therefore, their tiers will differ. For example, in an agreement, it may be that tier 1 is the lowest acceptable committed volume, which might be 20%, all the way through tier 15, in which you have 80% to 90% committed volume.

The definition of committed volume is that the supplier must realize sales from the health system of the defined tier percentage over a given period to achieve access to the price. The price is usually a rebated price, and in that case, the price is not realized until the rebate is paid. The rebate generally is not paid until after the measurement period, when the volume of sales percentage is validated by the supplier.

Often, the percentage of sales required by the agreement is not achieved, so the rebate may not be paid, and the price discount offered in the tier is not realized. The result is that the health system pays a higher price than the tier they selected allows.

These "all plays" are complicated agreements to administer and made more complicated by many variables after execution of the agreements. For example, often, there are new product introductions and product deletions from the category after the execution of the agreement that must be incorporated into the compliance and tier models. Factor this by multiple suppliers, and multiple agreements, as well as multiple tiers for as many as 5,000 hospitals, health systems, and non-acute providers.

In these agreements, tiers are structured such that the member's pricing gets better as the percentage of committed volume gets higher, notwithstanding the rebate structure presented above. Note that volume commitment is usually based on the percentage of market share of the member health system's purchasing in the category, not necessarily on a particular number of units purchased.

3.6 Health System Advantages in Strategic Sourcing

A hospital or health system has the ability to align, consolidate, standardize, and rationalize much differently from a GPO because they are able to bring all physicians in a category together for input on product performance, supplier representative performance, and the differences among manufacturers and products related to quality and service. To illustrate the difference in credible aggregation abilities on this scale versus the GPO's so-called "aggregation" model represented above, consider the process and results achieved by SharedClarity.

SharedClarity had one price for all member health systems, members agreed in advance, and aligned around their ability to achieve the high level of volume commitment. Also, that commitment was based on the membership's collective aggregation, rather than being based on individual member health systems such as when an agreement has multiple tiers. SharedClarity members agreed that 80%, or greater in some agreements, of their total volume as an organization would be committed to a reduced number of suppliers, again, resulting in agreements with a single tier representing one price for all.

A large GPO, because of the vast quantity of member health systems, is not able to get all of its members to agree in advance to a singular commitment of 80% or 90% with one or two suppliers in a category, such as cardiology or orthopedics. Thus, they are dependent on all-play agreements, a multiple-tiered commitment and pricing approach for each health system to select from, which also allows a GPO to maximize its admin fee revenue.

Again, the tiers represent that one hospital or health system might choose to commit 80% of its volume to a supplier, and another hospital or health system may agree to 40% commitment of its volume to a different supplier and so on until all GPO member health systems have made selections to the suppliers under contract in the category. These health systems will likely sign multiple tier selection documents with multiple suppliers in the same category such that they may agree to 20% commitment with supplier 1, 40% commitment with supplier 2, and 20% commitment with supplier 3, leaving the remaining 20% commitment to negotiate a local agreement with a supplier that may not have been awarded a GPO agreement, such as a "niche" supplier, or possibly a partial line supplier.

Notwithstanding this example, we have many times seen health system supply chain leaders sign 80% commitments with all awarded suppliers, taking advantage of the best possible price until suppliers figure out that their volume commitments aren't being met for this reason. The result is a price structure that is seriously diluted by volume that is spread out across a pie with many very thin slices, and a level of distrust between the suppliers and the GPOs.

Aware of this issue and the unfavorable impact it has on supplier pricing, GPOs have allowed their members to negotiate locally, and, or form local/regional aggregation groups to improve on the GPO agreement pricing. More on that later in this chapter.

Again, there is a fallacy in the industry that GPOs have gone through a structured strategic sourcing process such as we defined so far in this book. Instead, GPOs for the most part create these all-play agreements, revealing their inability to align, consolidate, standardize, and rationalize. In its place, they settle for an ability to provide contract coverage as a substitute. Rational thinking should conclude that if all suppliers or most of them in a category are on contract, a structured strategic sourcing process would be foolish and not required. The foolishness in reality is in the weakness of the outcome.

3.7 Will the Real "Paying Customer" Please Stand Up

A GPO's resulting lack of value is a testimony to their desire for revenue overriding their ability to create a model that delivers on their promise of "aggregation" as understood when the U.S. Senate secured their safe harbor, guaranteeing their revenue. The 1987 Anti-Kickback Safe

Harbor Statute (42 U.S.C. § 1320a-7b) allows GPOs to charge suppliers an administration fee (admin fee) of generally at or below 3% of the dollar volume of sales from the supplier agreements they negotiate. They are able to negotiate that admin fee into their supplier agreements at the best rate possible (usually up to 3% in accordance with the safe harbor) and at the same time create the tiered pricing that fits the complement of suppliers awarded in the category.

Health systems own the purchase order. That is important in this context, because they are the paying customer. As such, they're also making commitments on volume aggregation within their health systems. This commitment is made one health system at a time rather than being aggregated by the GPO and being built into the value proposition of an agreement.

Keep in mind here that each GPO-awarded supplier must visit each GPO member health system to compete with every other supplier awarded an agreement in the category for percentage volume commitment. This is different from the SharedClarity example where with one price for all, price activation occurred without the additional local and regional competition that occurs in GPOs because only one or two suppliers were in the agreement awards, and there was only one tier, or price for all health systems. From the supplier's perspective, being able to make volume commitments and delivering on those commitments is analogous to "owning" the purchase order.

As we presented in our previous book, *Implantable Medical Devices and Healthcare Affordability: Exposing the Spiderweb*, there are four things that truly matter to suppliers when negotiating an agreement:

1. How much volume do you represent?
2. How much of that volume can you commit?
3. How quickly can you attain that volume commitment?
4. Can you sustain that volume commitment throughout the term of the agreement?

We must note that with each level in the four questions above, if one can provide the answer that the supplier requires, price will get substantially better from question 1 to question 4.

Because of the large membership volume of a GPO, they have not demonstrated their ability to get aligned on those four attributes with all their members, and they lose significant value as a result. We will detail this "Earned Price Model" in Chapter 6.

3.8 Locally Negotiated GPO Contracts

Of utmost importance to a GPO is that the health system is using the supplier agreements they negotiate. The GPO agreements may provide the opportunity for a marginal price advantage, but this is not the critical point. The concept of "locally negotiated" value explains what we mean.

So, if the health system is able to extract better pricing than the best tier (it qualifies for tier 15 for example), and the supplier is willing to negotiate a better price option for tier 15 so that they can get quicker closure on securing 80% market share before one of the other "all-play" competitors—also a GPO-awarded supplier—is able to secure business, the member health system and supplier will negotiate this locally and directly.

Sometimes, the member will conduct a tier 15 price bid, putting each "all-play" supplier in the position of creating a better opportunity and then selecting based on that outcome. After the member health system selects their supplier(s) of choice from the GPO all-play supplier selection list, the supplier(s) has the health system GPO member sign what is called a *member designation form* (MDF), sometimes referred to as a primary member designation form (PMDF). This form is a local form, and a local agreement between the selected supplier and the individual GPO member that is attached formally to the GPO agreement.

This is a "price activation" agreement that commits the GPO member to that, or those suppliers at agreed-upon volume commitments and price, and activates the price for loading into the members' and suppliers' pricing systems. If there has been a locally negotiated price as indicated above, that new price will be reflected on the PMDF when activated by the member signature (Note: The member can sign multiple MDFs with as many awarded suppliers as they choose at various commitment levels.)

In almost all instances where new terms and conditions are negotiated, including the price section of the GPO agreement by the health system member, either the member will also negotiate that the admin fee will still be paid to the GPO as a condition of signing the PMDF, or the GPO has covered that an admin fee will be paid on "all sales," even when local negotiation occurs between the supplier and health system member. The GPO agreement will usually also require the supplier to not take the member off the GPO paper and onto its own agreement. It is important to know that the health system member is not a "signatory" to the GPO agreement.

The signed "parties" to the agreement are the GPO and the supplier. The health system is provided access to use the agreements through a contracted membership with the GPO and is allowed authority—either formal or informal—to renegotiate portions of the agreement by the GPO, usually through the MDF process.

3.9 Regional/Local GPO Formation

Regionally or locally, GPOs form sub-GPOs. GPOs, let's use Vizient and Premier as examples, will have all their member health systems on membership agreements, and a GPO roster. After signing a membership agreement, the health system is usually a member of that GPO through the term of the agreement. GPOs will often refer to their membership as "voluntary members." Of course, health systems choose to belong, or not belong; however, this isn't the primary meaning of the word "voluntary." In this sense, GPOs will describe that if a member doesn't want to use a particular agreement, product, or service of the GPO, they are able to "opt-out" voluntarily.

We see this happen from time to time, but it's not the norm. So, in the larger GPO—where volume commitment to the GPO supplier agreements is voluntary—thus the process of tier selection as described above—individual members may also form sub-membership groups or have sub-GPOs within the larger membership which may operate within the GPO but differently from the entire membership. One of these differences may be their ability to aggregate and commit to volume in the GPO/supplier agreements.

For example, a GPO such as Premier may get together with its member health systems in Delaware, Maryland, and Virginia and formally establish or recognize another aggregation group, or even a GPO legal entity. Although it is under the umbrella of Premier, suppliers and this regional group may negotiate their own terms and conditions regionally. This could be with clinical items and/or nonclinical items. They may want the suppliers to use certain warehouses or logistics channels, or besides the pricing, they may want to make local requests of the supplier.

Another example is a well-established regional commercial GPO. The Greater New York Hospital Association (GNYHA) now known as Healthcare Leaders of New York (HLNY) operates one such GPO. GNYHA, founded in 1904, represents 280 hospitals and health systems in New York, New Jersey, Connecticut, and Rhode Island, and possibly has affiliate members in other states such as Pennsylvania. This is an example of a nonprofit organization that has created a GPO as part of its services to its members that operates under its own organizational structure and management but has created an agreement with a national GPO in part to bring its membership's volume under the umbrella of the national GPO (Premier Inc.).

3.10 Where is the Strategic Sourcing Relationship?

The intimate relationships for collaboration that are essential to conducting true strategic sourcing do not exist in the GPO/health system sourcing models today. There are reasons why this is true, and we will be presenting these as we move forward. First, we need to address the practical facts. It is not practical to expect that a major GPO, such as Premier Inc. for example, can be embedded effectively with every member in the 4,400 member hospitals it represents for the purposes of strategic sourcing. Do they have field representatives who meet with internal stakeholders periodically and are assigned territories that include the member health systems?

The answer is yes, but these representatives are not assigned for the purpose of getting strategic sourcing alignment with all internal stakeholders so that the entire membership can become aligned around a strategic sourcing strategy that could rationalize, consolidate, and standardize suppliers and products. Additionally, GPOs such as Premier Inc. and Vizient would tell us that abiding by their decisions about which suppliers to buy from is voluntary. As such, they have said that they don't block or prohibit new market entrants from selling into their member health systems with or without a GPO agreement. GPO agreements generally leave as much as 20% open to these choices to allow physicians the opportunity to utilize the all-play GPO agreements while still being able to choose nonagreement suppliers.

Vizient is as large, or larger than, Premier, and as a third example, Health Trust Performance Group would have similar issues being embedded in all of their member hospitals. The GPOs will insist their members are embedded in their sourcing strategies. However, just consider the examples in Chapter 2 and the beginning of this chapter of strategic sourcing in one category alone, and it will become evident that the strategic sourcing process the GPOs refer to must be seriously diluted and abbreviated for them to be able to make this claim.

Additionally, as mentioned above, there is a "second" sourcing process that takes place locally and regionally once GPO agreements are executed. This process in large part is a recognition of the fact that the

GPOs are not only unable to embed, but are also unable to align in aggregate with all of the many thousands of their hospital members, especially around volume commitment and value with the health systems' internal stakeholders.

The second sourcing process is an attempt by the local and regional supply chain executives to accomplish this internally within their individual health system. More evidence of the GPOs' inability to aggregate alignment are the "all-play" agreements and the multiple tier structure within each agreement, as we have already mentioned.

The GPOs' current sourcing process results in a majority of health system members not seeing what has been committed on their behalf by their GPO until the negotiations are complete and the agreements are signed. This is primarily because only a small subset of health system supply chain leaders who serve on the GPO committees have the privilege of seeing these agreements in the making, and they are usually under a nondisclosure agreement (NDA) with the GPO. The NDA usually allows them to speak with their own health system stakeholders about the agreements "in-the-making" but nobody else. These conversations may have a limited audience.

The GPOs will assert that they have category managers and clinical people on their own teams, sometimes including physicians and nurses. They will also say that they're connected or embedded with the health systems because they have committees, consisting of physicians and nurses from the member hospitals, that provide input.

The problem is that they may have committees made up of a mix of nurses and physicians or other clinicians, but they don't get down into the institution and acquire alignment clinically where it matters most. That is, their committee members bring knowledge and experience into the selection process but representing all other clinicians and physicians in the health systems as if they have provided input and buy-in once selections are made is absent. In a high-functioning strategic sourcing process people should be working together on strategic sourcing solutions daily and communicating up and down the organization in each health system that would be required to use a supply agreement.

The process lacks the rigor it requires at the local or regional level when the GPO is in control. The committees usually meet once a month, usually by video conference or by phone. The committees may meet roughly twice a year face to face, and so the ability to touch each other and communicate is much more limited than it would be in what we have described as effective strategic sourcing.

3.11 Where Are the Gaps That Prevent Effective Strategic Sourcing?

In this chapter we have laid out how sourcing plays out generally in U.S. healthcare today. In the next chapter we will outline three major gaps that are interfering with our ability to conduct effective evidence-based value analysis and strategic sourcing, as we introduce what we call "The Lacuna Triangle."

References

Anti-Kickback Statute. (1987). *Criminal penalties for acts involving federal health care program.* Social Security Act § 1128B [42 U.S.C. § 1320a-7b].

Thomasnet. (2023). *Cardiac pacemakers suppliers.* Thomas Publishing Company. www.thomasnet.com/products/cardiac-pacemakers-55540306-1.html

Chapter 4

The Lacuna Triangle: Gaps form Barriers to Strategic Sourcing

The U.S. healthcare system has been plagued by gaps that get in the way of quality outcomes and lowering healthcare costs—gaps between the siloed departments in hospitals and health systems, gaps in the continuum of care for patients, and gaps between those who can afford care and those who cannot. In the supply chain there are gaps between physician engagement and supply chain relationships, knowledge and appreciation gaps concerning the interests of physicians, C-suites, supply chains, and suppliers, data, studies, and more.

We are calling attention here to what we are branding as the "Lacuna Triangle." Lacuna is defined as a gap or perhaps more fitting in this context, an unfilled space, and those gaps cause true strategic sourcing in healthcare to get hopelessly lost. We believe there are three major lacunas in the U.S. healthcare supply chain strategic sourcing system that are preventing us from creating what we consider a successful strategic sourcing process. These are intentionally locked in the Lacuna Triangle, and they prevent us from detaching from our current processes and becoming independent from the GPO and supplier shackle. Understanding these three lacunas could go a long way toward addressing those listed in the previous paragraph, and more.

DOI: 10.4324/9781003495291-5

The Lacuna Triangle includes three major points of disengagement:

■ A talent disadvantage
■ Blind acceptance of physician preference items
■ Lack of strategic alignment.

These three gaps create an almost total lack of leverage for health systems considering creating successful, independent, and aligned strategic sourcing processes. These major points of disengagement form the dangerous "triangle of prevention" where unknowingly and unwittingly health systems have lost control to the GPOs and suppliers who work in tandem to maintain a tight grip on the barriers of the triangle walls.

This was not a strategy created by the GPOs or suppliers, but an uncalculated, fluky, and random occurrence that neither the health systems nor the GPOs contemplated or considered as today's supply chain ecosystem developed over the past 25 years. But it must be considered now, because the Lacuna Triangle is the primary cause of value loss when considering a well-managed, high-performing, and aligned strategic sourcing process and its intended result. The suppliers' heavy influence on physicians, health systems, and GPOs, in addition to the GPO stranglehold over health system supply chains and strategic sourcing processes must be reprocessed back into the health system's primary influence. Remedying these unfilled spaces is the way to get there. Let's look at the three points of the Lacuna Triangle.

4.1 Lacuna #1: Talent at a Disadvantage

In our first book we touched on the meaningful talent gap between suppliers and the GPOs and health systems, in which both GPOs and health systems are outmatched. To be clear, we are not talking about IQ or lack of education or experience. In our healthcare supply chain experience we have worked with some of the most talented and loyal professionals in any industry. Our comments are centered around an issue of the financial and personnel resources that can be wielded, and in this respect, the suppliers have the greatest advantage. GPOs are also outmatched by suppliers in this regard, but they still also lead health systems in financial and personnel resources dedicated to supply chain issues.

There are several reasons we have a talent gap in healthcare. It starts at the grassroots level where leaders in other industries proactively recruit professionals out of leading college supply chain programs, offering internships and valuable developmental rotational programs for new hires. Such practices are much less common in health system supply chain management.

In industries outside of healthcare you are recruited fresh from college as a supply chain analyst or supply chain associate, or whatever title they give you. As a new recruit, you might spend 6–12 months in a warehouse, then in purchasing, and then maybe in materials management for example. Such a rotation provides practical experience on the inner workings of the supply chain department, while allowing the associate to build their own network within the enterprise before settling into their first full-time role.

For example, let's take Conagra Brands, headquartered in Chicago, with 18,000 employees, 42 manufacturing facilities, and $11.5 billion in operating revenues. It is known as a "consumer packaged goods" organization. You will recognize the company from its food brands, which include such well-known names as Birds Eye®, Duncan Hines®, Healthy Choice®, Marie Callender's®, Reddi-wip®, and Slim Jim® (Conagra Brands, 2023a).

For comparison to healthcare, if Conagra Brands were a health system, in terms of revenue, it would not even make it into the top 10 among health systems in the United States (Definitive Healthcare, 2023). Despite this, Conagra Brands has a robust program to onboard new supply chain associates. The company says its Supply Chain Development Program is structured to last 36 months, and it rotates associates through three appropriate supply chain functions, offering some of the following growth opportunities based on the individual's career aspirations:

- Running a variety of scheduled reports and providing supporting analytics
- Managing procurement master data in logistics and enterprise resource planning software systems to help drive process efficiencies
- Building cross-functional relationships
- Supporting enterprise process improvement and documentation
- Developing an understanding of cost drivers and market dynamics
- Collaborating with marketing and finance on monthly consensus volumes and translating those volumes to lower levels to finalize the mix of volume
- Developing future plans to drive process in the supply chain
- Analyzing existing shipping processes for improvements and providing support for a variety of implementation plans

- Providing leadership, and resolution, to the company and customers on supply chain issues
- Being trained with "lean" and "agile" skill sets (Conagra Brands, 2023b).

Unfortunately for those in healthcare, in many of the college supply chain programs, the curricula relate mostly to manufacturing. The focus is often not on service entities such as hospitals and health systems. Still, a person with a degree in supply chain management, even with a manufacturing focus, is much more valuable than someone without one. However, we would argue that running the supply chain for a health system or Disney World is a great deal more complicated than the supply chain for a Honeywell or GE or Honda.

With a Honda facility you have one product and one production line. You know many months out which cars are running through, you have a defined bill of materials with product specifications, and you understand everything that is supposed to happen to get those cars to the end of the production line in good working order and done in an operationally and financially expedient way while assuring the highest quality. And you have a good idea how many of those finished products you are making and how many feature variants you will have to produce.

In a hospital or in Disney World, you don't know what the next customer who comes through the door or gate is going to do. With a hospital they could be experiencing an abnormal heart rhythm, or they could have a broken leg. At Disney World they might buy a hat they saw on a character in one of your movies or golden slippers from another one. They might buy these items from an amusement park or an online store. One Disney patron could be ordering a bunch of hot dogs for the family during their visit, while another buys multiple boxes of fudge out of a shop to give as presents to friends and family back home.

Additionally, in both the hospital and at Disney, the products needed to support these efforts have a shelf life and are frequently being discontinued and replaced with newly released products. You just don't know how demand may shift. Service industries can be much more of a challenge in that respect.

In healthcare the major strategic sourcing roles are watered down. This is because the GPOs have part ownership and significant influence in that process. As we saw in the Conagra example, from the very beginning, high-performing strategic sourcing professionals in other industries have opportunities to gain experience in the following:

- Developing and leading cross-functional teams
- Aligning and influencing people around strategies
- Negotiating both with internal customers and outside suppliers
- Developing wide internal and external industry networks
- Becoming known throughout the industry.

Not having exposure to that breadth of experience and opportunity is a symptom of that watered-down role, and it is not good for professionals who want a meaningful career path in supply chain management. The second problem it creates is in compensation, and it is not as if health systems cannot afford to compensate a good CSCO well. As we pointed out in Chapter 1, with healthcare spending quickly climbing toward 20% of GDP, the money is available. Healthcare does not pay supply chain leaders as well as other industries, again, in large part because if the GPOs are seen as providing many of the functions of the supply chain leader, then that position carries less value in the minds of the decision leaders.

Healthcare supply chain salaries may be an indication that health system C-suites acknowledge that the GPO admin fee is a cost. When health systems look at the costs of having the GPOs perform their strategic sourcing operations, paying their own supply chain people can seem like an added, or even redundant, expenditure. The true problem is that the money is being spent in the wrong way—on admin fees rather than on talent.

In many cases, hospitals and health systems hire supply chain people from within their own systems, or within the industry, partly from a belief that the healthcare industry is unique. For example, a nurse might make a seemingly logical progression from a clinical role to being an analyst and then on to a category manager. In a strategic sourcing environment, in some ways, that can be a good thing, because having internal people familiar with the physicians, suppliers, and product categories is valuable. Internal promotions could come with an investment in development and education of supply chain best practices as seen in the most successful health systems, as well as in other industries, in order to broaden the knowledge base of the employees being promoted. Conversely, it can serve to further inhibit the infusion of new talent and new ways of thinking into the healthcare supply chain.

Another talent issue is the career ladder for supply chain personnel in healthcare. Supply chain, strategic sourcing, logistics, and materials management personnel in other industries are frequently promoted to other executive-level operational roles, including chief operating officer, general manager, business unit president, and even chief executive officer.

In healthcare in the United States, even if the organization has a CSCO position, the CSCO is rarely promoted into COO or hospital president roles. We say "in the United States" because the same is not true outside the United States. As one example, while working for UnitedHealthcare Global, we traveled to UnitedHealthcare-owned hospitals outside the United States to perform our duties. We met some amazing healthcare professionals in South America and Europe. At Hospital Lusíadas Lisboa in Lisbon, Portugal, we saw in two of that system's hospitals supply chain executives who had been promoted to CEOs of hospitals, and in one case, a former supply chain executive is CEO of the entire health system.

The result of all of this? Health systems are disadvantaged in attracting exceptional supply chain talent into their organizations. This is not a criticism of healthcare supply chain personnel but a reflection of the factors mentioned above.

GPOs are not a good breeding ground for talent growth opportunities either. Largely, the GPO top-tier management and their inner circle are populated with healthcare consultants, healthcare product, or service sales leaders from outside of health systems and not hospital C-suite talent. Many of the entry level entrants are recent college graduates within the discipline they work, such as IT, pharmacy, or nursing programs. Furthermore, the mid-management talent is generally those who have been promoted from within the GPO from entry-level positions. In some instances, nurse talent is hired from hospitals, but the transition from patient care to a business role or a strategic sourcing role can be difficult for many nurses. Generally, GPOs have "no-poaching" agreements with their member hospitals, and those agreements make it difficult for them to hire embedded healthcare talent.

To change this there needs to be a primary and immediate focus within healthcare on the processes, techniques, resources, and education curriculum mentioned above expanded at university levels and within healthcare corporate structures. Also, as CSCO positions open up, consideration should be given to a balance of legacy people and people from the outside. For example, having a makeup in the supply chain organizations as two-thirds legacy people and one-third people from outside of healthcare.

In making this kind of transition, the organization can keep its knowledge base of people who know healthcare, and it is not seen as cleaning house. You are simply bringing in enough people with fresh perspectives, knowledge, and talent who can help your existing crew pilot solutions that work in other industries. This is especially critical with the goal of eventually moving away from GPO influence, because those "outsiders" understand the value of being the primary influencer with suppliers and internal stakeholders and aren't saddled with a dependency on GPOs, while the "insiders" have the experience edge when it comes to working with internal category managers and other internal customers.

4.2 Lacuna #2: Blind Acceptance of Physician Preference Items

Physician preference in healthcare is often looked on as a product category. We would define it not as a category but as a product selection criterion that has been accepted for so long as a category that it is possible most people who work in the supply chain today are unaware of why the term was coined, and how long ago it became unknowingly accepted in healthcare as a term representing scientific evidence. Some in healthcare have gone so far as to create a definition of "physician preference" that states: In the absence of studies that prove without a question of doubt that empirical evidence has been found, "physician preference" will become that evidence (Burns et al., 2018).

In healthcare we find that many of those who study cause and effect issues that plague the industry are those who largely have not spent time being responsible for a health system's profit/loss statement, budgets, physician, or supplier relationship, nor is it likely that they worked in a health system supply chain in any capacity. Yet they are called upon to deliver expert testimony, commission and conclude studies, and write articles and books on topics well beyond their practical experience base.

One must consider how this accepted status quo might be manipulated to the point that quality and cost are not considerations. Why would manufacturers of competing hips, knees, cardiac stents, or pacemakers/defibrillators, for example, want to expend efforts trying to determine patient outcomes, cost, and quality if a physician can claim their preference is evidence of scientific quality, possibly leaning heavily on statements, or comments, such as the physician preference "definition" above? Then, if the government allows payments to physicians for assistance in product development and to speak publicly about their preferences, techniques, or practice habits without a full, independent "follow" of the patients being treated to determine quality of care, cost, and outcomes, possibly everyone (except the patient) benefits. So, is it possible that physician preference is accepted so blindly that we allow it to drive costs significantly higher on products for which we have no scientific evidence of differentiation?

Physician preference has become over the years such an accepted term that many equate it to scientific evidence. How it most often works in hospitals and health systems is that, in the absence of what we would call empirical evidence in the value analysis process, we look to physician preference as the opportunity to make selections, and that physician preference becomes a definition of quality.

If this situation does not upset anyone, perhaps what follows might. In a study of the physician's understanding of proven experience and views of their professional expertise, the authors refer to physician preference as having the ability to tailor scientific evidence to any particular situation at hand where scientific evidence exists—in effect, overriding it (Dewitt et al., 2021). This is a flawed assumption that creates a flawed process. These physician preference items become part of the strategic sourcing process, but they are anything but strategically acquired. What use is scientific evidence in such a world? Why wouldn't manufacturers, who are aware of these opportunities, not exploit them to their benefit?

The physician preference item as a moniker came out of a process that has been in the supply chain for a long time. Before materials management information systems were so pervasive, and before we had GPOs dominating the supply chain processes of large health systems, there were standalone hospitals. We had a manual ordering process through the purchasing department, in which products were acquired, usually by purchasing agents, who managed several categories, including such categories as medical/surgical, capital equipment, biomedical engineering products, and more.

The operating room (OR), where surgical procedures occurred, usually stood alone and had its own purchasing agent who worked with the nurses and surgeons in the OR to understand which surgeries were happening in the next week or two. Using the OR surgical schedule, the purchasing agent would use a tool that was developed between the OR staff and hospital purchasing to keep track of the preference items of each physician specialist, including orthopedic surgeons, cardiologists, cardiovascular surgeons, interventional radiologists, and more, to easily keep track of common items repeatedly used in each surgical case to order supplies and products by physician/surgeon name.

These items were typed on what was called "physician preference cards" and filed in the purchasing office and the OR by surgeon name. So, when Dr. Georgulis and Dr. West, one being a cardiologist and the other being an orthopedic surgeon, had three surgeries next Wednesday, the OR would send preference cards to the purchasing agent with the quantities to be ordered based on patient load for that week's surgeries.

They were also the early basis for the development of something known by OR nurses as "custom packs."

Those preference cards that listed the preferred items of each physician/surgeon have morphed into what we have accepted as the physician preference items, or PPIs, as we know them today, and they have been built into our language and our acceptance of physician preference as scientific evidence of quality. The concept has also been digitized into our materials management information systems—same concept, but just a different format.

We present more about the effects of physician preference and PPIs later in Chapter 6, when we address strategies for how we can overcome the gaps they create. At this point, it is most important to know that studies have shown that PPIs constitute from 40% to 60% of a hospital's total supply costs (Burns et al., 2018), and much of it in the present day is driven by interactions between suppliers and physicians, which complicates our efforts to achieve effective strategic sourcing. It must be mentioned here that a good deal of today's problems are based on decades-old standards that run up and down a health system. For example, prior to value-based care and accountable care organizations, high-cost items created high-charge items. This was predominantly a "cost plus" reimbursement environment. As a result, service lines became sacred and protected by CEOs and CFOs. Those service lines were dominated by PPI products and the physician specialists who implanted them adding to the "mystique." These interactions are also one of biggest reasons for the third and perhaps most significant gap that impedes strategic sourcing: lack of alignment.

4.3 Lacuna #3: Lack of Alignment

The first two lacunas, or gaps, in our ability to provide effective strategic sourcing—talent and physician preference—are significant contributors to the lack of alignment in the health system enterprise.

When supply chain leaders are mere order takers on product selection committees and we accept that a significant number of very high-cost products on our shelves are PPIs, there is currently no place in the organization for the kind of EVA that drives the high level of alignment needed for true strategic sourcing. In fact, "evidence-based value analysis" might be skewed so far away from real evidence as presented in the prior section where opinion or preference by a physician can be a determination of scientific evidence, that the value analysis outcome might be more determined by opinion than empirical evidence. This is a serious flaw in the process.

EVA was at the core of the business model when we created SharedClarity, and it should form the foundation of any healthcare CSCO's strategic vision for their supply chain operations. The goal of EVA is to gain intelligence on how products perform, and to provide data to support product selection decisions, while improving patient outcomes and reducing costs.

In healthcare strategic sourcing, EVA forms the first half—consolidating, standardizing, and rationalizing products—of the strategic sourcing process. Without it, there is no second half—going into negotiations with suppliers with the leverage of committed volume backed up by full alignment.

Together, these find the optimal solution to meet the financial, operational, and clinical needs of the enterprise. When preference or opinion overrides science with or without the presence of empirical evidence, there can be no real aligned foundation. This point is the fallacy accepted by the industry allowing manufacturers to control the selection process and prices without competitive difference in performance and outcomes.

EVA is the greatest opportunity for the healthcare supply chain to become the locus of alignment from the bottom to the top of the enterprise and stand out more than any operational unit in the organization in that regard. For this opportunity to be realized, the supply chain organization within the hospital or health system cannot be seen as some traditional departments might—conducting its business walled off and siloed from the rest of the enterprise.

Unfortunately, in many health system enterprises, this is the case, with the supply chain personnel mostly concerned with common traditional supply chain management metrics tied to fill rates, stock outs, inventory turns, cycle times from requisition to receipt, and inventory levels. These traditional metrics are the big umbrella over which supply chain operates, and they are crucial to strategic sourcing's ability to monitor, anticipate, and adjust to the needs of the enterprise, but they are inherently transactional. Strategic sourcing is primarily concerned with cost savings and the spend under contract.

4.3.1 Hard Lessons on Alignment from the Suppliers

As we hinted at above under the talent disadvantage section, coordinated teams of highly educated, experienced, well-resourced people from the manufacturers/suppliers are constantly working with health system and

GPO organizations. The operative word here is "coordinated," which speaks to their high level of alignment, not only throughout their own organizations, but within the health system. They have been provided a defined mission by their leadership. And the way they accomplish this mission provides a lesson in alignment for healthcare supply chain leaders and other top leadership in their own enterprises.

Supplier alignment starts at home—up and down their own organizations—where their personnel learn and are provided intensive training on proven strategies in a wide range of applicable skills, including in the following:

- Data and analytics
- Negotiation principles, tactics, and strategy development
- Behavioral observation
- Contract planning and execution
- A powerful, deceptive process of contract disintermediation.

Because of these skills and the talent gap we detailed above, the people on these supplier teams are often molding and persuading under-resourced and underinformed health system and/or GPO personnel on negotiation techniques as they are in the process of negotiating with them. This creates a level of trusted guidance and acceptance within the organization and the supplier representatives they are negotiating with, which leads to alignment. Not an alignment that's based on a CSCO-built strategy providing for the clinical, operational, and financial improvement of the health system, but one that aligns with the supplier's objective and suits the supplier and GPO category strategy. For the reasons we detail in the next paragraphs, everyone gets to live in peace.

Long before they begin negotiating with the organizations, supplier representatives have been aggressively aligning physicians with their products. In the case of the IMDs we highlighted in our first book, device manufacturers/suppliers have developed deep relationships with implanting physicians often from the beginning of their careers, offering inducements that health systems struggle to compete with, including the following:

- Speaking engagements with honoraria at national and international conferences
- Exclusive use of the latest technology
- Opportunities to conduct research and obtain research grants
- Technical support on the specific devices during surgery.

Often, these incentives are too cumbersome and/or too expensive for the health system to provide on its own—especially that last tech support piece—so they relinquish that benefit to the supplier to handle. This effectively makes that particular manufacturer's device indispensable to that physician, which complicates the standardization, consolidation, and rationalization process, to say the least. It severely hamstrings the effort to convince physicians to change devices as a result of a supply chain-driven EVA process or to even get physicians involved in that process in the first place. This is in part an illustration of the contract disintermediation process that suppliers use if a contract happens to be awarded to a competitor and not them.

Another of these benefits where health systems can't compete with suppliers is offering speaking engagements, which can gain physicians not only notoriety and stature in the medical community but an often-significant source of side revenue as well. The second and third inducements above—giving physicians the first crack at using new technology and offering research opportunities—can not only be a boon for the physician but for the health system the clinical provider works for in terms of marketing and promotion, and thus new business.

All of these offerings for physicians demonstrate the alignment lacuna between the suppliers and the health systems/GPOs, with the highly aligned and resourceful suppliers solidifying their own alignment at the expense of the provider organizations' ability to effectively align within their own supply chains. Because GPOs and health systems haven't seriously addressed strategies to counter this alignment ability of suppliers, we see higher cost all-play agreements. Thus, peace in the halls and C-suites of the hospitals!

4.4 Gauging the Effects of the Three Lacunas

The three gaps of the Lacuna Triangle (see Exhibit 4.1) work together to almost totally take the health system's leverage away when it comes to being able to successfully deliver the benefits that strategic sourcing processes can provide. That is, they are standalone gaps, but in the context of the Lacuna Triangle, they cannot be addressed separately. Together, they represent one problem for health systems. For example, if the talent gap were to be addressed and a solution found, the other two lacunas, if still in existence, would pose as deep a problem for effective EVA and alignment as if the talent lacuna had not been addressed. All three must break free of the walls of the Lacuna Triangle if self-reliance is to exist for strategic sourcing in health systems.

Figure 4.1 The Lacuna Triangle—the Hiding Place for Poor Outcomes

GPOs have had a hand in creating the talent and alignment gaps by "taking some of the load off" supply chain personnel and narrowing their role within health systems. Also, the fallacy we mentioned earlier—that the safe harbors GPOs operate under creates value—helps all-play supplier contracts proliferate and contributes to problems we see in all three lacunas. Suppliers also have contributed significantly to the talent and alignment gaps through their alignment with physicians in order to drive PPIs and with executives in order to get around the supply chain. Also contributing significantly to alignment gaps is blind acceptance of physician preference as scientific evidence, rather than forcing independent studies that result in a true scientific assessment of physician technique, product performance, and patient outcome results.

Suppliers, physicians, and GPOs have found a surreptitious hiding place for the lack of product performance and outcome differences, which is a major contributor to their high-profit margins. Where is that "hiding place?" Inside the Triangle under the cover of the operational disfunction they have created in the three lacunas! And while they did not create the term *physician preference*, they have been successful at "professionalizing" it and getting suppliers, physicians, supply chain leaders, and hospital executives comfortable with it to the point that acceptance isn't even questioned and using it to drive prices up is customary and conventional.

4.5 Three Gaps, Three Effects

The three gaps of the Lacuna Triangle bring about three effects that have damaging impacts on the industry. The three major deleterious effects the Lacuna Triangle creates are as follows:

- An oligopoly
- Pricing irrationality
- Irrational markets.

Lacuna Triangle Effect #1: Oligopoly. When GPOs create "all-play" agreements like those we detailed in Chapter 3, suppliers are operating in a "multisource" environment where, in any particular category, the GPO's hospital members would be able to select from multiple suppliers. The suppliers, for the most part, are okay operating in this environment. They are not potentially disadvantaged compared to their competitors because most health systems are likely to choose multiple tiers that, overall, deliver higher price points per unit. Also, knowing the tiers in the GPO agreement gives suppliers the intelligence—a "license to hunt"— they need to allow them to openly walk into the health system with their own proposal for the C-suite and the supply chain. Without this market intelligence they would not be able to be so brazen. For decades, this situation has helped to turn the market for high-end medical devices and capital equipment in healthcare into an oligopoly, where relatively few sellers are available in the market and there is a high bar to entry for up-and-comers.

Lacuna Triangle Effect #2: Irrational Pricing. The prices for goods and services in all GPO contracts are nearly all within a few percentage points of each other. Only 1% to 2% of health systems change GPOs in a single year, largely because there is virtually no differentiation in pricing. Suppliers are complicit in this because it is not in their interest in this ecosystem to bring overall prices down, and there is no incentive to do so. Why would suppliers want to change the status quo when they can be in a contract in which one health system is paying 50% more for that supplier's drug-eluting stent because of the tier structure?

Lacuna Triangle Effect #3: Irrational Markets. This issue is a spin-off of the oligopoly effect and irrational pricing because it creates the lack of a need for healthy competition, resulting in an irrational market in which suppliers don't really compete with one another on price, but rather on market share that is often based on a flawed impression of product quality and performance. Suppliers are comfortable in the oligopoly ecosystem and its lack of pricing differentiation. Instead of competing on price, they are competing on market share. The all-play agreements also take away the need to compete by differentiating the quality and performance of their products based on independent, evidence-based, and scientifically rigorous analysis of those products, creating the assumption that market share *is* the evidence. Physician preference bolsters this misconception that market share translates to quality and preferable health outcomes.

4.6 Moving Forward with Strategic Sourcing

Some, especially among suppliers and GPOs, might argue that the EVA process of consolidating, standardizing, rationalizing products could stymy competition. But we would argue that the "all plays" of GPOs actually stymy competition by making it unnecessary for suppliers to compete on unbiased differentiation and quality, safety, and value. Making suppliers accountable promotes healthy competition. Look at other industries—the automobile industry for example. Watch their commercials. They are all about quality, durability, safety, and value.

Remedying these gaps takes a commitment to true strategic sourcing and that begins with demonstrating the value of doing so up and down the enterprise. In the next three chapters we will present a best practice strategic sourcing model, along with tools and advanced strategies for conducting evidence-based value analysis.

References

Burns, L., Housman, M. G., Booth, R. E., & Koenig, A. M. (2018). Physician preference items: What factors matter to surgeons? Does the vendor matter? *Medical Devices: Evidence and Research, 11,* 39–49.

Centers for Medicare and Medicaid Services. (2022). *National health expenditure projections 2021–2030*. U.S. Department of Health and Human Services. www.cms.gov/files/document/nhe-projections-forecast-summary.pdf

Conagra Brands. (2023a). *Overview*. www.conagrabrands.com/our-company/overview

Conagra Brands. (2023b). *Destination Conagra* [LinkedIn jobs page]. www.linkedin.com/company/conagra-brands/jobs/

Definitive Healthcare. (2023). *Top 10 largest health systems in the U.S.* www.definitivehc.com/blog/top-10-largest-health-systems

Dewitt, B., Persson, J., Wahlberg, L., & Wallin, A. (2021). The epistemic roles of clinical expertise: An empirical study of how Swedish healthcare professionals understand proven experience. *PLoS One, 16*(6), e0252160. https://doi.org/10.1371/journal.pone.0252160

Chapter 5

A Best Practice Strategic Sourcing Model in Healthcare

5.1 Getting to Alignment

In the previous chapter we closed our Lacuna Triangle with perhaps its most important gap—the lack of alignment of health systems in comparison with suppliers and GPOs when it comes to strategic sourcing. We have been consistently emphasizing the power of alignment in achieving our strategic sourcing goals. In this chapter we will address how to design the strategic sourcing process to align your end user, your C-suite, and your supplier.

Alignment is pivotal when creating a best practice strategic sourcing model in healthcare, and the ability to implement effectively requires support from the very top levels of the enterprise, especially the CEO. Accomplishing alignment throughout the enterprise involves weaving together three elements we have not detailed yet in this book:

- Having committed supply chain resources embedded in the departments of internal customers
- Understanding and committing to the operational, financial, and clinical needs of the enterprise

DOI: 10.4324/9781003495291-6

■ Creating an environment where internal customers, peer departments, and suppliers are like-minded.

This chapter presents four foundational elements or tools that create this necessary organizational alignment:

■ Rigorous evidence-based value analysis (EVA) processes
■ Category strategies
■ Supplier business reviews
■ Physician research.

5.2 Adding the "E" to Value Analysis

Rigorous internal health system EVA processes require involving physician leaders, the C-suite (remember this includes the CSCO) and the leaders of clinical and business units of the enterprise, and a supplier component. The leaders of those units are not necessarily active daily participants, but their buy-in is essential in providing access to their staff and information resources. That information item is as important as access to the personnel, because in EVA, transparency is also paramount. Quality, safety, cost, outcomes data, and analyses among departments must be freely shared, and the analyses must be comprehensive. We should acknowledge that supplier product information must be brought in during the EVA process, while recognizing that suppliers are not part of the EVA team.

All this openness can be unnerving at first, especially in organizations where silos have historically been strong and where the supply chain has been seen as merely the order-taking function of the enterprise. However, it is essential in EVA, especially when it comes to physicians. Remember, our biggest problem with the physician preference lacuna is that physicians are the ones who choose the products that will be used with—and often *in*—their patients but they frequently make these selections without considering the effects of those choices on costs which they are generally not held accountable for.

A big part of aligning physicians with EVA that enables consolidating, rationalizing, and standardizing products down to one or two suppliers is achieving affordability that is quantifiable and measured, which directly supports the cost-savings validation process. This means aligning those efforts not only with financial statements and budgets but also with the patients' ideal result of not paying a ton of money in out-of-pocket costs.

Speaking of physicians and alignment, executive leadership in the organization must first align its EVA and sourcing strategy to go hand-in-hand with its physician-retention efforts. This is a dilemma, because the C-suite needs to commit to EVA in such a way that it can overcome the inherent risk of physician dissatisfaction that comes with nurturing the physician preference selection to include improved clinical outcomes and financial performance.

Physician alignment in PPI selection is a delicate dance in the EVA and sourcing process that is a one-off in healthcare and has no parallel in the supply chains of other industries. One-offs don't exist where alignment occurs. However, it is critical to overcome this disruption for two reasons:

1. We don't want to lose our physicians to other health systems because of process or product selection dissatisfaction.
2. We need physicians at the very top of our EVA process, leading the charge for change.

We will present much more about advanced strategies for overcoming this challenge in the next chapter.

Aligning the organization around strategic sourcing begins with a Clinical Effectiveness Committee created by executive leadership and led by a chief medical officer or other top clinical leader. Subcommittees of this lead committee are divided by product categories and are led by category managers, who are chosen from top physicians in clinical specialties related to those categories. To guide the work of these committees, we use two foundational tools: category strategies and supplier business reviews.

5.3 Infusing the Category Strategy Mindset into the Enterprise

The leadership of a healthcare provider organization must entrust category managers to strategically lead and implement procedures and protocols for how all goods and services—clinical and nonclinical—are evaluated, sourced, and provided to the enterprise. The expectations for these managers are no different from what is asked of department chairs and hospital presidents. Effective category managers align with the organization's formal strategic planning process, which explains where the organization is at and where it is going in the future. It is as if they are running their own business inside the enterprise. Category managers manage categories strategically. That is, with a plan at the center of the category, which is built, monitored, maintained, and executed by the category team.

Category strategies are formally documented and periodically updated, so they are evergreen. If you search "category management strategy template" on the internet, you will find many good examples. The ideal template for a category strategy would include several components, and they should answer the following questions at a minimum:

- Who is in the market?
- What are their capabilities?
- What are the cost breakdowns for the products?
- What products are being bought?
- What products are being bought and not utilized?
- What is in the new and upcoming product pipeline?
- What products are being deleted or becoming unavailable?
- Who are the influencers and decision makers?
- Who is on their team and ours?

Effective category strategies require foundational knowledge of the following:

Goods and Services. This knowledge includes specification and/or statement of work, the stock keeping unit (SKU) list, and how the products or services work, including their functionality and features. We also want to know how they are made, who manufactures them, who uses them, what the benefits are of using them and are there differentiated benefits among competing like matched products, what are the cost drivers associated with them, and what products are lining up in the product pipeline. All of this information is critical in looking for and evaluating competing products against one another.

Current and Forecasted Needs. For this element we need to know the purchase history of each product or service in the category by SKU, supplier, and facility. We also need to determine the forecasted volume by SKU, supplier, and the unique requirements of the item, including issues such as shelf life and delivery constraints.

Industry Profile. We need to have a comprehensive overview of the market in a given category. This includes a list of all potential suppliers with detailed profiles, and a market strengths, weaknesses, opportunities, threats (SWOT) analysis of suppliers. We also need to be continually aware of new entrants in the market and supplier manufacturing and delivery capacity.

Internal Decision Makers and Influencers (Category Team). Looking inward, we need to know and involve the people who use or consume the goods or services and who have budgetary responsibility for them. As we have emphasized throughout the book so far, that knowledge means learning and committing to their operational, financial, and clinical (or nonclinical) needs.

Goods/Services and Supplier Selection Criteria. These criteria are set by the category team and, again, are based on the operational, financial, and clinical (or nonclinical) input and needs of the enterprise. The criteria should be as objective and quantifiable as possible. For example, selection criteria can include the product having specific functionality and features, defined delivery standards, access to technical support within a specified time period, and financial thresholds.

Selected/Nonselected Products and Suppliers. This goes back to maintaining the list of suppliers and the characteristics of the products and to the selection criteria above. It is helpful for the category team and the EVA teams to keep a record of which goods and services were both selected and not selected and why. Supplier and product lists should also denote all product substitution options. While doing this, a plan should be formulated for which nonselected suppliers to maintain a strategic relationship with.

Current Supplier Contract Portfolio. This information includes which suppliers are currently under contract, how much the enterprise spends with them, and when their contracts expire. As a side note, the enterprise contract calendar must be considered in this process. This also contains information from the supplier business reviews, which we will detail later in this chapter.

5.4 Strategies and Tactics in Category Management

In achieving success in category strategies, efforts must align with the financial, operational, and clinical/nonclinical needs tied to that good or service. For example, in orthopedics, this may mean supporting the goal of reducing orthopedic hip replacement procedure costs by 10% within a year. In radiology, this may mean reducing delivery lead times and reducing on-hand inventory by 30% on products that have less than a 10-day shelf life.

Strategies around supporting these efforts include creating a consolidated statement of what the category team wants to accomplish on a macro scale. For example, consolidating suppliers overall by 50% with the goal of improving affordability by at least 25%. This might also include something such as reducing the source-of-supply and product inflationary challenges by helping bring in two to three new market entrants that add at least 25% more manufacturing capacity into the industry. This goes back to being good stewards of the markets.

On the tactical level, good category strategies employ action plans, which lay out how we will achieve the overall category strategy. These include plans for both strategic sourcing and contracting timelines, supplier business review schedules, and schedules for affordability and quality projects.

Category strategy buy-in and alignment flows throughout the organization. To align around the category strategy, the category team signs off, literally and figuratively, on the strategy document, allowing C-suite and functional leaders to lend their support to the category strategy process. Individual and department goals are also aligned. An example might be that the cardiology department has a goal to reduce knee replacement procedure costs by 10%, while the cardiology category manager has a goal to reduce cardiology implant costs by 10%.

As in any combination quality/cost improvement effort in healthcare, measurement is critical to success. The key metrics that are tracked in these efforts, again, are aligned with the needs of the enterprise. This means that they are usually items of high financial and/or clinical impact.

Category teams deal with a range of issues, including supplier lead times, on-time delivery, product recalls, product change/add/delete management and, of course, cost savings. They periodically present their category strategies to the CSCO and other appropriate functional leadership, which might include the orthopedic department chair, a hospital president, the vice president of enterprise-wide facilities, and others. This all helps to further alignment around strategic sourcing throughout the organization.

You may notice that in this presentation of category strategies, we have spent little time addressing supplier negotiation and contracting. That is because, while they are important parts of the category leader's responsibility, they are two activities among many within the category strategy effort. That effort sets the stage for well-informed supplier negotiation and contracting with research and evidence on products, and knowledge of product and supplier performance in the context of the needs of the enterprise.

When category strategies are documented and accomplished well, they make it easy to quickly onboard new colleagues into the process, refresh those who may require it, and move easily into the next cycle. Category strategies and the process it takes to effectively develop and implement them help establish the culture of the enterprise, which, in turn, drives alignment around strategic sourcing.

5.5 Supplier Business Reviews and Physician Research—Keys to Alignment

The work of category strategy teams includes research into outcome and cost trends for both clinical and nonclinical products. In these efforts, we rely on two primary sources: supplier business reviews and physician/clinician research. Let's start with supplier business reviews, one of our foundational tools.

Some might consider these reviews to be a performance review for the supplier, but we consider them to be more as part of the agreement, and the relationship in that the review is a two-way process. In other words, it's a performance review on the relationship the agreement has created. Suppliers are continuously introducing new products to the industry and more directly to clinical staff, including nurses and physicians. The business review can be an update on that process, but also covers many other purposes, some of which we'll detail below. This is a living process, constantly ongoing.

The purpose of supplier business reviews is to maximize the suppliers' contributions to the enterprise from the perspectives that matter most to the organization. The current practice within healthcare is that the hospital or health system leaves it to the GPO to conduct this process. Outside of healthcare, where GPOs do not dominate, companies are self-reliant, conducting the supplier business review process internally, led by supply chain management.

Supplier business reviews usually focus on suppliers that have a significant impact on the enterprise's financial, operational, quality, and clinical success. Business reviews should be conducted with these key suppliers in meetings two to four times per year.

The thoughtful selection of the staff who attend these meetings is important to the success of the review process. Attendees may include the following representatives from the enterprise and supplier:

■ Enterprise Side—category leader, category team, and others invited as needed. Depending on the subject involved in a particular review session, this might include physicians, facilities leaders and/or staff involved with clinical effectiveness, accounts payable, distribution, and more.

■ Supplier Side—national or regional account representative, key local sales representatives, and others invited as needed. This may include customer service representatives and people in product development, depending on the focus of the specific business review.

The following are some of the topic areas that are commonly covered during a supplier business review:

■ *Contract Compliance.* Discussion may include issues and opportunities for improvement.
■ *Metrics.* Delivery schedules, price discrepancies, recall response, product mix, and other issues may be discussed.
■ *Current and Upcoming Industry and Market Trends.*
■ *Other Trends.* These could include discussions of price, raw material availability, new market entrants, and more.
■ *Company Updates.* Personnel changes, expansion efforts, and operational changes might be discussed.
■ *Supplier Product Pipeline Issues.*
■ *Studies/Research Efforts.* Physicians and representatives of appropriate facilities might participate. Visibility into the upcoming product pipeline could also be addressed.
■ *Product/Service Feedback.*
■ *Operational/Administrative Issues.*
■ *Joint Project Status.* This could be updates on affordability, growth, process improvement, and more.
■ *Current Agreement Issues, Concerns, or Activities of Interest.*

The topic list above is often a driver of where a given meeting might be located and who will attend. Some meetings may call for touring certain facilities and talking with specific department or team personnel. An example might be introducing and hooking up product research team personnel from the health system with product development staff from the supplier. Another could be having customer service representatives from the supplier visit a hospital that has service issues with the supplier.

Supplier business reviews provide innumerable opportunities for finding ways to grow the suppliers' business, improve pricing, collaborate on new product development, gain commitment to certain delivery and service levels, and clarify contract commitments. They also help clarify and refine metrics for the health system for its performance measurement activities by meeting on those metrics and identifying outliers.

Stakeholders on both sides of these reviews frequently walk away with action plans for improvement so that both parties are living up to the terms and conditions of the contract. Most importantly, these reviews help create and maintain that sense of alignment among health systems and suppliers. We, on the healthcare provider side, are assuring the supplier that we are meeting their expectations for business, and they are assuring us they are meeting our financial, operational, and clinical needs.

To maximize and maintain the relationship between the enterprise and the supplier, these meetings need to be conducted without GPO involvement and at the local level. Speaking of GPOs, they are a supplier to the health system and should also be required to participate in frequent business reviews to measure their performance and contribution to the enterprise. Supplier business reviews are a vital component of alignment around strategic sourcing. They are one of the best foundational tools to help health systems become self-reliant and accelerate affordability, quality, and performance.

5.6 Physician Research Aligns EVA

Another foundational tool is physician research. In addition to being caregivers, physicians are scientists, and they are conducting research, both locally and across the globe. They are interested in what is new and what is possible, and in terms of what this book is about, they care about the health outcomes of the patients they provide care to, so many of them are engaged in measuring it. Many have been engaged with suppliers throughout their careers, some on a nearly daily basis. This is one of the reasons why we want physicians embedded in our value analysis processes, especially from a category leadership perspective.

But it does not stop there with those two primary sources of research. Other sources include analyzing system outcomes data available through the organization's enterprise resource planning system or other internal studies on the products' outcomes. They also research existing studies in the literature, and available quality and safety information on the products. Another source of information is conversing with other physicians in outside organizations who have experience with these products.

Remember that we are striving to evaluate the products and services the hospital or health system buys to make sure each item provides the optimal solution for meeting the enterprise's needs.

This is not only for complex lifesaving (and potentially lethal) products such as the implantable medical devices we focused on in our first book. The enterprise also buys thousands of other products it does not make, whether it is slippers that help ensure patients don't fall in the hallways, or gloves, gowns, and masks to protect our workers from infection.

So, how slip-proof are those slippers we are buying? How well does the personal protective equipment we are buying protect our workers from infection? And what are we paying for those products? While these products might not be physician preference items, do we possibly have a blind "preference" problem with these items as well?

With nonclinical items, the evaluation is different. There may not be as much, or any, scientific research and studies so you might be conducting field testing of products and services. You may be going to competitors to learn about their experiences with supplier performance or conducting internal surveys on this issue.

The result of this committee effort in clinical effectiveness is to get to clinical consensus on the efficacy of the products.

At the same time, supply chain personnel have a committee structure that is nearly identical to the EVA committee model and is led by the CSCO or other high-level supply chain executive, but this is a strategic sourcing committee. As in the clinical effectiveness committee, the subcommittees are organized by product categories, and supply chain personnel and departmental budget stakeholders serve together on them. The strategic sourcing committee and its subcommittees base their work on the findings of the clinical effectiveness committee to develop sourcing strategies that align with the clinical, operational, and financial needs of the enterprise.

Both committees collaboratively evaluate and potentially source new products coming down the pipeline in the various categories and work with suppliers on quality issues, new products, and possible opportunities for health system clinicians involved in EVA to participate in and/or conduct research on upcoming products from the manufacturers.

5.7 The Value of Value Analysis Leadership

Value analysis is the cornerstone upon which healthcare strategic sourcing for clinical products is built. Again, we prefer to make the distinction that what we are referring to is *evidence-based* value analysis because most often that first critical "E" element in EVA is either left out entirely and, or equally as horrible, it is replaced with blind acceptance of physician preference.

When speaking of the EVA process inside a provider organization, it includes physicians, nurses, and nonclinical healthcare professionals who have the benefit of a network of like-minded and aligned peers they can communicate with throughout their organizations. In an enterprise that employs EVA, these professionals are aligned for much deeper reasons than the fact that they are all employed by and acting on behalf of the same provider organization.

The EVA process is in stark contrast to what happens with GPOs when they choose products and services for their member hospitals and health systems. In a large GPO, the value analysis team usually consists of several experienced clinical nurses who depend largely on 25 to 30 member clinical nurses representing thousands of hospitals and health systems, with possibly one or two physicians working with them per category. The physicians on these teams are usually brought in for specialties, as in a radiology or cardiology agreements. However, in most national GPOs, there might be only two or three physicians on a committee representing all their thousands of member organizations.

The clinical nurses and physicians who work within or with the GPO are very capable, credible, and able. However, their limitation is that they do not and cannot reach the entire GPO membership of clinicians and physicians in a way that aggregates their alignment as it should be if they were truly working to drive "value." And they are not end user decision makers when it comes to implantable devices and many other products, such as surgical instrumentation and pharmaceuticals. The "analysis" part of what they do has merit.

Most health systems have their own operational value analysis committees. These may act as new product committees as well, so the committees are not only looking at existing products, monitoring the quality and what value those products are bringing, and whether they should be on the shelf or not. They also assess products in the suppliers' pipeline and help inform physicians and nurses of new product opportunities coming soon from various suppliers.

Consider two types of supply chain strategic sourcing people that are on these committees:

■ One is a subject matter expert who is highly engaged and seen as part of the leadership of those value analysis committees. They have clarity and understanding around what meets the quality standard, doesn't meet the standard, or is a physician preference. They can constructively challenge and align the committee on scenarios to consolidate toward high-performing products and improve quality and affordability.

- The other sits on the committee taking orders while the physicians decide which products the hospital or health system is going to use, and then, they ensure those products are available on the shelf.

In healthcare, generally that first type of supply chain participant is the exception rather than the rule. The first type takes on leadership and collaborative roles—communicating and having constructive influence with the physicians, building relationships and knowledge credibility, ensuring there is a process of alignment of product selection by looking at longitudinal studies, or other science related to the products, and making logical, research-based decisions that form the basis for sound and collaborative consolidation and rationalization decisions.

"Order takers" don't provide the leadership that delivers value in health system supply chains and patient care environments. Hospitals and health systems need leaders with deep understanding of strategic sourcing and a committed strategic sourcing perspective, working through a process that is vetted and thorough. Order takers take the "value" out of the value analysis process.

So, when a value analysis process doesn't begin at an aligned health system level, the ability to get the value out of the value analysis process is minimized.

5.8 The Strategic Sourcing Skillset

In high-functioning healthcare enterprises, the strategic sourcing leader owns the sourcing process from top to bottom through strategic vision, design, and creating category strategy partnerships with physicians, suppliers, and internal leaders to find the right collaborative, long-term solutions for the enterprise. This requires a skillset that includes the following:

- Strategic planning
- Effective communication
- Keen focus on process
- A collaborative mindset
- Business acumen
- Executive presence
- Negotiation expertise
- Project management
- Understanding clinical (and nonclinical) needs of the enterprise.

Communication, Ability to Influence, Collaborative Mindset, and Clinical Understanding. If we are to close the physician preference lacuna in healthcare strategic sourcing that we detailed in Chapter 4, our supply chain professionals must have communication skills, the ability to influence, a collaborative mindset, and deep understanding of the clinical needs of the enterprise in their toolbox. In many hospitals and health systems today, manufacturers and suppliers maintain sole or primary relationship strength with key physicians such as cardiologists, orthopedists, radiologists, neurologists, pathologists, and nursing staff. These clinicians are instrumental in selecting products in the categories such as implantable devices and major medical capital equipment, which are important to organizational leadership because of their high cost. Supply chain personnel need to use effective communication, influence, and collaboration skills with the clinical side of the enterprise to insert themselves and put that alignment back into the organization where it belongs. This should be accomplished in a way that doesn't alienate the manufacturers but collaboratively includes them in the alignment process.

Business Acumen. In order to take that C-suite alignment back from suppliers, supply chain leaders must be able to influence annual departmental budget processes, especially where capitalized, high-cost clinical products or equipment are involved. To do this, they must possess a high level of business acumen, which is defined as *knowledge and skill informed by experience.* Healthcare organizations can help develop this knowledge, skill, and experience early through the type of onboarding and professional development programs we presented in the previous chapter and will present in the next chapter when we address advanced strategies for strategic sourcing. These programs can include immersion in financial and data aspects of the enterprise, as we presented in the Conagra Brands onboarding model in Chapter 4.

Executive Presence. Part of the executive presence aspect is creating an environment in which the supply chain leader rather than the C-suite or the GPO manages the suppliers' sphere of influence within the health system. Trusted clinical and physician relationships that supply chain leaders should develop would serve to displace supplier or GPO dominance and cultivate influence with key participants inside and outside the health system.

Negotiation and Process Focus. As we will see in detail in the next chapter, negotiation, like EVA, is a process. Supply chain leaders can only gain an appreciation for this process through experience. This is one reason the onboarding process for new supply chain associates fresh out of college is so important. They need immersion and mentoring from experienced negotiators from the beginning of their healthcare experience. The onboarding process that the supplier/manufacturer negotiators experience includes these important elements and leaves the health systems at a serious skill disadvantage. This is part of what created the talent disadvantage lacuna we presented in the previous chapter.

This chapter laid out some of the foundational elements of a high-performing strategic sourcing model. In the next chapter we will offer several advanced strategies for bringing rationality to an irrational market in not only both pricing but in how we choose products and manage our relationships with suppliers.

Chapter 6

Strategic Sourcing Advanced Strategies

6.1 Bringing Rationality to Supplier Pricing: The Earned Price Model

Being able to demonstrate reductions of between 30% and 50% in costs for products in specific high-value categories as SharedClarity did took more than addressing the foundational elements we covered in Chapter 5, such as supplier business reviews, value analysis, and analyzing quality and outcomes data. When we get into the actual "sourcing" part of the equation, we bring in the advanced strategies that are needed to create high-performing strategic sourcing processes.

Remember from earlier chapters what the ideal situation is for the supplier: They want 100% of a product (or capacity to provide a service) already committed in sales as it comes "off their production line." Suppliers know that one customer alone is not able to satisfy this ideal so what they want from each customer is as close to 100% of their purchase volume to be committed sales. If the supplier is confident they have assurance of this from a buyer, they will do amazing things when it comes to what we call their "plan B price," including putting it right up front in the negotiations, which is where you want it.

Strategic sourcing is about satisfying mutual interests between the buyer and the supplier rather than one entity getting a leg up on the other. So, using our knowledge of what suppliers value most, we developed a

DOI: 10.4324/9781003495291-7

concept called the "Earned Price Model" whereby we get to an optimal price by doing our best to earn it. After all, is it possible for a supplier to say they wouldn't want a customer who asks to earn their price? At SharedClarity we wanted a single optimal price, rather than a multitude of suggested tiers. We also knew that to get there we had to demonstrate we could deliver to suppliers the four elements they desire most in getting to their overarching goal. These elements are the pillars of our Earned Price Model:

- Volume
- Commitment
- Speed
- Sustainability

To convince suppliers that we could deliver on those elements in any category, we developed four questions from the supplier perspective, the answers to which determine and demonstrate our dedication to that model:

1. How much volume do you represent?
2. How much, or what percentage of your volume can you commit?
3. How fast can you achieve that high percentage of volume?
4. Can you sustain that commitment through the full term of the agreement?

By having the right answers to those questions and following through with action on those answers over time, we were able to demonstrate to suppliers that we could accomplish all four of their most prized elements, while other aggregation groups weren't capable of the same.

In addition to the model described above, and its pillars, suppliers are measuring strategic sourcing people on their credibility, reliability, and reputation. When the four questions above are presented to suppliers, and a discussion on how and why you, as a strategic sourcing professional, can deliver, a measurement of your credibility, reliability, and reputation will be taken by the supplier. You will either stand alone on these three characteristics or be put in a category with the "others" who might have been able to check some of the boxes, but they couldn't deliver on them all.

Some organizations represented more volume than SharedClarity but fell short when it came to committing a high percentage of that volume they represented. In other words, they are unable to aggregate their volume as one customer. Suppliers will value a higher percentage commitment of volume over total available volume as a price driver, because they work to control a larger market share than their competitors. Suppliers will also value current business loss at a higher priority than new business gain.

Some aggregators could promise a high percentage of commitment, but may not have been able to fully deliver or could not make it to that level quickly. SharedClarity worked to meet its volume commitments within a 90-day period after execution of the supplier agreement. Others might have been able to gather the volume and commitment in a timely manner but were not able to sustain those levels through the life of the contract.

"Earned" is the key word in the Earned Price Model, because it's where credibility, reliability, and reputation are built. Exhibit 5.1 demonstrates the difference in where committed aggregation groups land in the Earned Price Model versus where most others are. Most others are defined as aggregation groups without commitment. Without commitment, aggregation is a fallacy and suppliers aren't fooled.

That last element of *sustainability* is critical, because the *earned* in the Earned Price Model means that an aggregator or large health system (which in essence *is* an aggregator) must demonstrate to the supplier that they can sustain their commitments from the implementation of the contract to its end. If suppliers are not assured that hospitals and health systems can sustain their commitments, then there is nothing to entice them to meaningfully reduce the prices of their products.

Figure 6.1 Earned Price Model

The current "all-play" free-for-all in the GPO world guarantees the furtherance of the irrational pricing and unbalanced supply markets in healthcare that we touched on in Chapters 1 and 4. If you are a typical supply chain leader in healthcare today, you are working with the GPOs and trying to make an irrational market work without doing anything to fundamentally change it. You are attempting to manage an unmanageable yet accepted situation in which physicians select products but have no financial responsibility for the consequences of their selections, where there is no independent quality and outcome data, where GPOs establish inflated industrywide price benchmarks to support their admin fee growth, and where you are paying a premium for unproven products.

We believe committing to the Earned Price Model all the way through the sustainability element can help bring rationality to the current irrational pricing market that has been created by suppliers and GPOs creating agreements that meet their own needs at the expense of the health systems that depend on them. If hospitals and health systems are consolidating, standardizing, and rationalizing based on unbiased real data, and then using authentic strategic sourcing under this model, it would spur healthy competition among suppliers in a given category on quality outcomes and price.

The concept is simple: All customers should "earn" their best price based on their ability to deliver commitment in aggregate as one.

6.2 Advancing Your Relationship and Becoming a Customer of Choice

There are other leverage points that can be employed that enhance the Earned Price Model's ability to improve affordability. One of them is being the customer of choice to the supplier. You differentiate yourself as a preferred customer. You do more than simply live up to the contract terms. You support their projects as and when you can, and you assist them in growing their business through the contract. This support might include research or studies that need a facility for piloting new processes or systems, introductions to clinicians and physicians, or assisting in finding a suitable facility and clinical team for new product introductions.

Suppliers care deeply about volume, and they know that the pathway to growth is with strong, positive relationships with a hospital or health system's doctors. This is especially true if your organization is a teaching institution. The suppliers greatly value the opportunity to assist in training your residents, fellows, and guest physicians. The suppliers know that if you are an orthopedic surgeon and early in your career you are trained with implanting Zimmer hips, chances are good that you will use Zimmer hips when you're out there practicing.

Where there are residency and fellowship training programs, the hospital or health system can quantify over the term of the contract how many residents, fellows, and guests physicians would be educated at their facilities using their products during their training. Being able to demonstrate such support can be a point of leverage for the health system because of the significant, decades-long revenue stream it can provide to the supplier.

This may happen in nonclinical areas as well. You may know from your relationship that the supplier is adding a new facility or trying to fill some volume in one of their manufacturing facilities to optimize their resources and keep their costs low. This is another area where the health system might provide support and further solidify that customer of choice status and provide leverage for more favorable terms on current and future contracts.

Another strategy is just being opportunistic, and this takes not only intimate knowledge of your supplier but also broad intelligence on the markets as well. An example, and GPOs understand this leverage well, is if you have a good supplier who just lost a big customer. That may be a good time to approach them and perhaps add a year on the back end of your contract and negotiate more favorable pricing. This is about addressing their need and helping your affordability needs.

Another opportunity along these lines might be that raw materials dropped in price. You're buying corrugated packaging materials and all of a sudden pulp markets crash, so you could possibly renegotiate in that area and extend the term of the agreement, again working together with the supplier and enhancing the relationship.

The point of striving to be a customer of choice is enhancing the relationship and having all suppliers recognize that a relationship with you has value beyond the agreement. And having them see that only delivers leverage if you maintain control of the ability to "put all business at risk" as is illustrated in the bottom line on the Earned Price Model.

All suppliers must recognize that you're aligned within your organization to such a degree that you can move business on a number of levels toward or away from them based on who is selected as a contracted supplier. One of the most powerful points of leverage with a supplier is the fear of losing a significant amount of business. Knowing that strategic sourcing professionals have the enterprise credibility to make business move from one supplier to another with the support of the physicians, clinical teams, and C-suite is the engine that makes the Earned Price Model deliver incredible results.

We don't want to make this sound like everything is playing hardball. Again, the ultimate health system/supplier connection is about building the relationship. When you have a contract, it must be built on credibility and trust. If you as a health system can't move the business so all suppliers understand that all business is at risk, the relationship doesn't matter.

6.3 Implementing Contracts So Suppliers Do Not Interfere

If you have ever taken on a task where carpentry skills are required and have gotten so frustrated that you decided to hire a carpenter to finish the task, it becomes evident quickly that carpenters have learned little tricks that get their job done quicker, more efficiently and with an outcome that we as amateurs could never achieve. Observing them do their work or working directly with them allows us to understand the value of those skills. The same is true about the actual *sourcing* part of strategic sourcing in healthcare. The process of negotiating category contracts with suppliers takes about a full year. During that time, the suppliers you are negotiating with are expending significant effort in developing relationships not only with you and your sourcing staff but with your nursing staff and the physicians, and if they already have existing relationships with them, they are working to deepen and strengthen those relationships.

The suppliers will take the time to go out into the hospitals and assess how well they are doing in terms of potentially winning business through the negotiations process whether it's with the GPO or the health system. They do that by going to the people on the committees related to nursing, physicians, and overall strategic sourcing, and they elicit feedback on how things are going.

So, suppliers are often in tune with what a negotiations outcome may be long before the negotiations conclude. This puts the strategic sourcing team at a disadvantage. What's worse is these activities by the suppliers aren't unknown to the strategic sourcing team. Barring the suppliers is impossible, however, because they use their need to speak with the committee members about other clinical issues as the basis for these discussions, and prohibiting their ability to follow up with the clinical staff on clinical issues can be detrimental to patient care.

There is a dynamic that we will introduce here that is helpful and should be understood. During the contract negotiation, 60 days prior to execution of the agreement until about 90 days after agreement execution, is a critical period that becomes pivotal in being able to execute the contract with awarded supplier(s) the way it is negotiated. Understanding this 150-day period and being able to use some sourcing "tricks" effectively can build credibility, reliability, and reputation. That 150-day period breaks down as follows.

6.3.1 Sixty Days before Contract Signing

Approximately 60 days before the health system or GPO is ready to sign the contract, suppliers know whether they are going to win an agreement or not. So, let's say you have seven suppliers engaged in the sourcing process, and you are going to award a contract to two of them. Those five that are not going to be awarded a contract already know they will not be likely to win, because they have been doing their due diligence. At about this 60-day mark, the two that are going to be awarded a contract have a good feeling about their chances for the same reason the others have a bad feeling about theirs.

Regardless of their status with regard to winning a contract, in this process all seven of them have created a plan B price that the strategic sourcing team is not aware of. The plan A price is the price they give to the people they are negotiating with. The plan B price is lower and developed as such to get under the contract price to compete with the awarded suppliers in case a supplier does not win an agreement. They drop their price to the plan B level in an attempt to either maintain their current business and/or win new business.

Suppliers know this price is below their current competitor because they have been in this process for 12 months, and they have good insight where everyone else is regarding price. They know that their negotiated price was "close" but may not have been the best. So that 60-day period is when those suppliers who know they're not going to win are out securing business with a better price than they offered the health system negotiator or the GPO.

This is where the suppliers become very disruptive in the current process as we have described throughout this book. They go to the doctors, nurses, and administrators in the hospitals/health systems and say: "I would have offered you a lower price, but they never asked. I got shut out before the negotiations closed." Or they come up with other reasons why they feel they were disadvantaged during the negotiations. However, in most cases, none of this accurate.

This 60-day period before signing supplier contracts is a critical phase, and it is time to accelerate internal discussions with EVA and category team members to reinforce the alignment around the strategic sourcing process, decisions, and timing to combat disruptive suppliers. For the suppliers, their biggest fear is losing business and the salespeople who are compensated to maintain and grow their book of business become hyperaggressive. Effective strategic sourcing leaders anticipate the supplier disruption and consistently help their colleagues prepare on how to respond to it.

6.3.2 After the Agreement is Executed

The 90 days after the execution of the agreement is when we were trying to ensure that we had the agreement implemented. If you don't start getting ahead of that process 60 days before execution, you will not be able to implement during the 90 days after. Our job as negotiators who understand this "supplier dance" is to get better than plan B pricing from those who would become contract awarded suppliers, because if we didn't, implementing an agreement within our 90-day window becomes impossible.

A GPO that has 2,000, 3,000, or 4,000 hospitals does not work within that 150-day window, nor the 90-day timeframe in implementing a contract. Multiple tier pricing, thousands of hospitals, and the MDF process prohibit quickly executing awarded agreements. They are working within a 180-day period at the quickest to a 12-month timeframe or more, so they can never get ahead of that plan B price. While at SharedClarity we considered all business converted to an awarded supplier and full commitments met as agreement executed. GPOs consider MDFs signed as awarded agreements executed.

The difference is one of market share conversion. For GPOs, MDFs signed are where the conversion process begins. While SharedClarity had the business converted to awarded suppliers within about a 90-day period, it takes GPOs sometimes 12 or more months to consider the MDF process complete. And it is that plan B pricing that gives the health systems the intel to conduct local negotiations, which extends the MDF process and can mean that a health system won't be converting business to a new supplier. In a five-year contract award, with business not converting for as many as 12 months, and commitment sustainability ending as soon as 12 months before contract termination, an awarded supplier gets about three years if they're lucky of agreement purchases from a customer. This adds to the increased price margin required by the supplier to make the agreement profitable.

At SharedClarity we earned our price because we were aligned, and because of that alignment, the suppliers knew that when we promised an 80% commitment, we would deliver it. So, they gave us their 80%

commitment price. We didn't have to play the plan B game because we had it in hand from the beginning. Earned price was seriously better than "plan B" price because there was credibility, reliability, and reputation behind it, and because alignment meant that the cost of sales was seriously reduced.

There was no MDF process for commitment. Suppliers didn't renegotiate with SharedClarity members. Conversions, where necessary, began upon execution of the agreement in most instances without interference from non-awarded suppliers.

Whenever we explained this to a supplier, they knew exactly what we were talking about. It took them about 24 hours to turn around pricing. They were surprised that we knew the game.

On the other hand, if you were in one of our member health systems and a non-awarded supplier came in and tried to white knight us at the 12th hour, at SharedClarity we were able to emphatically say "No!" because we were aligned and we were able to get the CEO and the clinical leaders to agree not to accept that proposal. It was the only way to create credibility and ensure we received best and final proposals from all suppliers in the future on our required timeline.

6.4 Removing PPI as a "Category" through Clinician EVA Leadership

In our Lacuna Triangle model that we introduced in Chapter 4, physician preference items were one of the three major lacunas or gaps that impede strategic sourcing. It is also a significant gap through which suppliers can go around the supply chain leadership to influence product selection and costs.

It may seem counterintuitive, but the best strategy we and many in healthcare have found for overcoming the very expensive impediment of PPIs in the healthcare supply chain is getting clinicians as deeply involved as we can in evidence-based value analysis in our strategic sourcing. Why? Because clinicians are scientists, and effective EVA efforts bring science into the strategic sourcing process. That is, in an unbiased scientific process where evidence exists that an implantable medical device outperforms another, they can see the deleterious effects that physician preference is having in high costs and less-than-preferable outcomes.

Because physicians care deeply about their patients' outcomes both professionally and personally, demonstrating the outcomes piece is important. When talking with clinicians about high costs, it is important not only to point out the bottom-line financial effects of PPIs on the organization but also the pass-along financial burden on their patients.

We know from our extensive EVA experience that clinician involvement is paramount, and top leaders in hospitals and health systems today agree. In a 2022 research article, global management consulting firm McKinsey & Company reported the results of a survey of 121 top U.S. health system C-suite and supply chain executives (Bowen et al., 2022). The authors of this study concluded from the survey that in high-performing organizations, "clinicians play an integral role in supply chain initiatives."

According to the McKinsey survey, this role includes the following:

- Managing supply use
- Suggesting strategies for selecting suppliers and contracting with them
- Contributing to reaching quality and financial goals
- Supporting contract term compliance (i.e., ensuring that the enterprise meets that "commitment" aspect of the Earned Price Model).

In the survey, health system executives were asked, "What are the critical elements of a high-performing supply chain?" Their responses were then organized into three categories: clinical engagement, goal setting, and data and analytics. Of the 15 significant answers, the three clinical engagement-related answers all ranked in the top four. They were as follows:

- Physician committees that drive contract strategy
- Dedicated personnel to engage with clinicians
- Core sponsorship by a chief medical officer.

The respondents to the survey stated that shortfalls that created barriers to high performance included informal clinician engagement versus involving them in formal committees, accepting clinician decisions without question instead partnering and debating with them, and "under-investing in personnel on the ground in hospitals who can develop relationships to support implementation of performance improvements, identify new savings opportunities, and provide a formal feedback loop to the supply chain function."

Again, the EVA process was at the heart of the SharedClarity business model, and we believe it should form the foundation of the strategic vision for any high-functioning supply chain operation. This process has at its core the sponsorship of a chief medical officer, as the respondents of the survey above suggested, with physician-led committees engaged in gaining intelligence on product performance and providing input that supports strategic decision-making, and drives improvements in patient outcomes and reductions in costs.

This clinician-intensive EVA process also informs the consolidating, standardizing, and rationalizing of products in the strategic sourcing process. It serves to align the financial, operational, and clinical needs of the enterprise and promotes the supply chain as the locus of this alignment based on science, as we presented in Chapter 3. Furthermore, this must be a "locally" driven process engagement—that is, at the individual health system level.

Why is this so important? Because it's the only way to get feedback from each physician into the process, as was accomplished at SharedClarity. Without this, alignment is only with the few physicians who are engaged in the process, such as what we have experienced in a GPO value analysis process or committee product selection process.

6.5 Becoming Stewards of Rational Supply Markets

We started out in this chapter talking about rationality in pricing. For example, if you walk into a Subway restaurant with a friend and you both buy three subs each, you will be charged a reasonable price, and there is rationality in the pricing. That means you are not going to pay three times as much as your friend for the same subs they just bought.

Conversely, in this section we are addressing the rationality of the supply market itself. When we talk about the supply market, we are referring to a segment of the hospital or health system's supplier industry. This could be orthopedic related products or janitorial services, for example. It could also relate to our earlier gas station example, which we will do below.

From a strategic sourcing professional's perspective, being a good steward of the supply market is making sure that market is vibrant, meaning that there is an ample number of suppliers and product options available within reasonable timeframes, good competition in the industry, and plenty of industry capacity that will continue to be able to serve the market. You are working to make sure that the supply market fits your profile needs and meets the needs of your health system.

Historically in healthcare it has been the GPOs who have taken the leadership role in being the stewards of the supply market, and this is an area where they have failed. The GPOs have sat by idly while some markets—medical devices for example—have consolidated through mergers and acquisitions to a level that has seriously restricted supply options. Or they have not worked to force new market entrants either within, or outside, the United States to flourish where needed. The GPOs have allowed the suppliers to offshore to a large degree; the personal protective equipment debacle at the height of the coronavirus pandemic is one of many examples of that offshoring problem.

Now, the GPOs are working on "resiliency," which is basically just ensuring product availability and onshoring or nearshoring—which some call reshoring—making sure that the products are closer to customers, suppliers, and patients. But they are the ones who either didn't recognize the potential harsh realities of watching a supplier market move offshore or didn't care. The end result is the same and has played out in a way that causes a lot of "scrambling" as a solution is sought. So, now the industry is relying on the GPOs who helped cause the problem for solutions.

This is where we look back at our gas station example. This would be no different from our situation of the four gas stations at the four-way intersection. We negotiate and then end up going with one of them. Then, let's say because of the effects of that, one of the other three gas stations goes out of business, and then, the other two gas stations merge, and they decide to close one of them. All of a sudden you have gone from having competition and a vibrant market in that area to a year or so later having only half the number of suppliers. So, when your contract is up, your leverage position will be much different, and your options will be fewer.

6.6 The Benefits of Simplified Pricing

In the second phase (after EVA) of the strategic sourcing process, which is the actual sourcing itself, the supplier relations piece is key.

In addition to the ability to meet all the objectives of the Earned Price Model, one of the advantages of a large health system managing its own supplier relations is inherent visibility into product costs in all of its hospitals. As a third party, at SharedClarity we were able to look at each member's prices, and we found that the suppliers found ways to mask the pricing, so that the price the health system believes it is getting might not be the actual price. This can happen especially when rebates are in the mix.

Rebates can be impactful as their discount percentages rise. For example, if you are working with a more full-line supplier, a medical device may be bundled with other products, and you will only receive a discount if you reach a certain volume level. But, if you buy that medical device and buy it along with three or four other specific products, frequently termed bundling, you will get another discount on those products (usually via a rebate). This clouds the product's acquisition price.

Consider also that rebates are usually based on meeting volume thresholds over an agreed-upon period. If those volume thresholds aren't met, the rebate is at risk either in full or partially. During agreement periods, health systems experience many product changes, adds, and deletes from their original product price list. This process, instituted by suppliers and written into GPO agreements, is another masking of the true cost of the agreement products. The change, add, and delete process may be a legitimate process, but it's also easily manipulated. This purposeful camouflaging of the price can inhibit benchmarking efforts to learn if your price is rational and reasonable.

Another way to shroud what discounts other customers are getting for their product is bundling-related disposable products in with capital equipment, so you are not always paying for the capital equipment. Using a nonclinical example, think of a high-end printer (the capital equipment), where there is no cost (or very low cost) for the printer itself, but there are charges for ink cartridges and weekly maintenance. In this example, the percentage add-on to the disposable product and the service charges help finance the capital equipment. In this example, the health system may never take ownership of the capital equipment, which could reduce asset inventory and depreciation opportunities.

This can also be true for capital equipment we see in the operating room or the labs. For example, hematology machines need reagents in order to get results for the patients, and these reagents can be priced based on the volumes that are used by the hospital or health system. Over time, the markup on the reagents can be used to pay for the cost of the capital equipment, masking the cost of the equipment.

Because of activities such as these, the real cost of the products is hard to fully know until the term of the agreement has been met. Hiding the cost of products through a rebate process and the change, add, and delete process prohibits real and accurate cost validation. A high-performing EVA and strategic sourcing process will bring back the health systems ability to validate costs.

This is why simplified pricing is so crucial. On a basic level, simplified pricing is just knowing what you're paying. We had experience with a major health system that had a dozen hospitals and many more regional medical centers, and each of them was able to choose different tiers with the GPO. For example, there was a drug-eluting stent from the same contracted supplier that had seven different prices across the enterprise. Then, there were rebates and bundling that further camouflaged the prices among the different facilities in the same health system. To further complicate the price accuracy issue, consider the new product adds and repackaging changes over such a contract term.

The simplified pricing we had at SharedClarity created the transparency that was necessary to allow the enterprise to reconcile cost savings to provide true validation. It also allowed us to effectively budget: We had a three-year contract for that drug-eluting stent at a single price for all SharedClarity hospital members. You could budget for that and hold people accountable.

The absence of simplified pricing creates chaos and confusion that allows prices to continue to creep, because you can't reconcile what you're really paying for an item until long after you have paid for it. Simplified pricing is a lynchpin for transparency, cost savings validation, effective financial planning, and holding people accountable for departmental budgets.

It comes down to credibility that your strategic sourcing efforts are truly achieving the financial and affordability goals that you have set. A common credibility killer for strategic sourcing people is that finance staff and department leaders (budget owners) don't believe the cost savings numbers. If they don't believe them, then they question the value strategic sourcing brings to the enterprise.

This book details the difference between supply chains in a well-performing environment, usually outside of healthcare where the supply chain leaders are members of the C-suite, compared to supply chains, usually within healthcare, where GPOs and medical device manufacturers have more influence over key participants, such as physicians and C-suite members, than the supply chain leaders do.

In a well-performing supply chain the key participants are aligned, all-play agreements written by a third party don't exist, multiple tier price selections for the same product by various purchasers within the same P&L don't happen, convoluted rebate programs don't exist, and a mature EVA process is accepted. In environments such as these, direct pricing prevails, and accurate cost validation is the norm.

In the next chapter we explore how to gauge the results of your EVA and strategic sourcing efforts, including cost savings validation techniques and getting at the real meaning of cost.

Reference

Bowen, B., Galceran, B. C., Karim, S., & Weinstein, W. (2022). *Optimizing health system supply chain performance.* McKinsey & Company. www.mckinsey.com/industries/healthcare/our-insights/optimizing-health-system-supply-chain-performance

Chapter 7

Gauging the Benefits and Results of Healthcare Strategic Sourcing

When SharedClarity had been up and running for a few years, we had already conducted some of our clinical reviews, and through our EVA process with our health system members, we had reached consensus on a handful of products. One of the first comprehensive review and strategic sourcing processes we conducted was for drug-eluting stents. We were able to demonstrate an enormous cost savings and then standardize, consolidate, and rationalize down to one supplier on approximately 80% of the volume.

At this time, we were also seeking to expand our membership to allow other health systems to participate beyond the four core health system customers. We would have been happy having seven or eight health systems as long as we were confident they would follow the same culture and processes we had established with the others. That is, a process of data delivery for use in clinical reviews and studies, and contract compliance once the EVA process was agreed upon.

One of these prospective members was a prestigious health system and academic institution on the West Coast. We spent considerable time with them analyzing their processes and trying to get a sense of where their supply chain organization was in terms of maturity and openness toward the type of systems we were striving to create.

DOI: 10.4324/9781003495291-8

When we went there to meet the head of supply chain, we had to go into the basement of the building, which tells you a few things right out of the gate. The gentleman in charge had been with the organization for about 30 years and had been running the supply chain for about 20 years at that time. This organization operated within the traditional supply chain practices that we have described here so far—working with a GPO, relying on physician preference, not aligned with the C-suite and the rest of the organization on evidence-based value analysis, etc.

When we would initially meet with some of these prospective organizations, including this one, we were trying to understand the value proposition, that is: If we brought in this new member, what value could SharedClarity bring to them? Part of that determination was getting their pricing and comparing it to what we were currently getting from suppliers for certain items.

During this process, we learned the health system was paying more than twice as much for drug-eluting stents than we had negotiated for SharedClarity members. We also benchmarked other items and those were highly priced as well, but the stent jumped out at us because there was so much of a difference. What they were paying was in the full retail range at that time. We were stunned. How could a prestigious academic institution, having the leverage of current and future physicians being trained on specific supplier products, while being an active member of one of the largest GPOs in the country, be completely out of touch on what fair market pricing should be for their health system?

It got us thinking about what this was costing the health system. In our analysis we found that the system's spend on physician preference items was unproportionally high as a percentage of total revenue. So, how much did this person cost the health system in his 15 or 20 years as its supply chain leader? If his spend was double of what it should have been for drug-eluting stents, it is probably double for many other items as well.

This health system had one hire that literally was costing them tens of millions of dollars per year. Over his career, they could have saved hundreds of millions or even a quarter billion dollars. Think of all the struggles health systems go through having limited funds and being forced to decide between safety, staffing levels, and capital purchases. Think of the pressure on the foundation to raise all that money they had to find to simply fund core operations when the money was hiding there in the organization—money that could have been used to improve the outcomes of patients and improve the lives of people in their communities?

Big changes were needed in the health system, and it's not as simple as firing that guy in the basement.

7.1 Proving Effective EVA and Strategic Sourcing

Best in class strategic sourcing, performed in an environment of complete alignment, can have an enormous positive impact on the operational, financial, and clinical success of a healthcare enterprise. It is perhaps the easiest way to improve profit margin without affecting headcount.

The shift to EVA and strategic sourcing requires a substantial culture shift, breaking through departmental silos. It requires levels of collaboration that are not seen in many healthcare enterprises. This cooperation and coordination are especially important in validating the benefits of all the efforts we have detailed so far in this book.

In this chapter we get down to providing proof of the positive impacts of our efforts or areas that need improvement. In most organizational supply chains in any industry, validating supply chain performance involves the use of a set of key performance indicators (KPIs). In healthcare, one of the most widely cited list of KPIs comes from the Association for Health Care Resource & Materials Management (AHRMM) of the American Hospital Association. AHRMM has a detailed dashboard of 32 essential KPIs that their health system supply chain members should monitor and track. These are covered in Exhibit 7.1

While most of these KPIs are essential and highly valuable for measuring supply chain operations, we believe there are two glaring categories of omission that are critical for tracking the success of robust strategic sourcing efforts. These KPI categories are as follows:

1. Realized cost savings
2. Employee experience and development.

It would make sense that these two categories of metrics would not included in the list below, given the current environment in which health systems largely rely on GPOs not only for their sourcing activities, but for many of the other functions that we believe supply chain sourcing teams should be leading and coordinating throughout the enterprise. They are also logical omissions for AHRMM, whose members include people who work for GPOs and whose events and programs are sponsored in part by major GPOs as well as suppliers.

As you may have noted so far, we're not writing about the prevalent environment today in the health system supply chain in which GPOs run the show for the most part, where real costs are camouflaged and difficult to track, and where the role of supply chain leadership lacks independence. We're addressing effective strategic sourcing done by the organization if

AHRMM Supply Chain Key Performance Indicators	
Finance	Supply Accounts Payable Supply Expense Per Case Mix Index Adjusted Discharge Supply Expense as Percent of Net Patient Revenue Spend Under Management Inventory Turns Supply Chain Labor Expense Per Case Mix Index Adjusted Discharge
Operations	Perfect Order Total Suppliers Per $1 M Nonlabor Supply Expense Percentage of Purchase Order Lines with Expedited Shipping Costs Supply Chain FTEs Per $1 M in Total Nonlabor Supply Expense
Patient Safety	Expired Products as a Percentage of Total Number of On-Hand Products in Inventory Recall Management—Closed Volume Percentage Rate Recall Management—Delayed Recalls Percentage Rate
Resiliency	Internal Requisition and Order Fill Percentage Rate Primary Distributor Backorder Percentage Rate Percentage of Items Stored in the Item Master with Identified Substitutes Primary Distributor Fill Percentage Rate Nonlabor Supply Expense Per Case Mix Index (CMI) Adjusted Patient Days (APD)
Data Standards	Percentage of Invoice Lines Received with a Global Trade Identification Number (GTIN) Percentage of Invoice Lines Received with a Global Location Number (GLN) Percentage of Items Stored in the Item Master Populated with a GTIN Percentage of Purchase Order Lines Sent Out with a GTIN Percentage of Items Stored in the Item Master Populated with a GLN
Environmental Sustainability	EPP Products as a Percentage of Total Office Supply Expense Recycled Products as a Percentage of Total Printing and Copier Paper Expense Percentage of Medical Supplies That are Reprocessed Linen Pounds Per Adjusted Patient Day Copy/Print Page Volumes Per Employee Waste Pounds Per Adjusted Patient Day

Figure 7.1 AHRMM Key Performance Indicators

Source: Association for Health Care Resource & Materials Management (2023). AHRMM Keys for Supply Chain Excellence. www.ahrmm.org/keys

it were able to break free from the confines of the Lacuna Triangle. So, allow us to explain and then flesh out these two missing categories.

7.2 Missing Category #1: Realized Cost Savings

The exclusion of a realized cost-savings metric seems to be an industry admission that, in the current healthcare supply chain ecosystem, getting a handle on true costs is just too hard. There is no real known validation process to measure realized cost savings when it comes to GPO environments. And without being able to validate savings, you have no way of knowing what your cost is. While GPOs continue to make macro level claims about how much money they are saving the industry, the only accurate financial results health systems should pay attention to is savings realized in their own financial statements.

As we have explained in previous chapters, the GPO contracts can be highly convoluted, and the process that they go through—not just with the tiers, but the change/add/delete processes of products during the contract cycle with a supplier—means that the products and price are always moving. That is, the "product price list" within any GPO agreement is constantly changing throughout the term of the agreement.

Accurately measuring realized cost savings is virtually impossible with GPO contracts. All their hospitals are signed up at various different tiers. And then there are product changes, adds, and deletes all the way through the contract cycle. Change/add/delete is an accepted process whereby suppliers can change packaging, delete products, and add different products to the agreement's product price list. And those come with different, and usually higher, prices than what was originally negotiated. There is a continuous wave of change going on through the three to five years of a contract. Additionally, the use of bundled rebate programs that provide incentives for health systems to grow their business with a supplier across all their products and services brings another level of camouflaging product costs. At the end, nobody really knows what it looked like in the beginning. The original baseline is incomparable to current utilization data for the purpose of calculating cost savings.

Consider the analogy of ocean waves: Every time you get a new wave, new and different items are introduced into the flow, bringing a different set of results. And when you can't fix from a baseline what your comparative cost looks like, you cannot then move forward five years down the road and know exactly how much you saved or spent.

7.3 Getting at the Real Meaning of Cost

In an aligned EVA process such as the model we are presenting in this book, the questions about cost and quality run deep.

In many organizations, the EVA processes that we have covered are replaced by physician preference. The EVA environment we operated in at SharedClarity standardized, rationalized, and consolidated implantable medical devices (IMDs) down to a few manufacturers.

Our "cost" included the price, and through our strategic sourcing process, we had good multihealth system comparable data on what the price for a given IMD was, and would be, throughout the life of the contract. We also had a good handle on what our health system members would pay for that IMD once the next contracting cycle came around. Additionally, we had internal and external research on the reliability and outcomes of that IMD that could help us project other costs that might be incurred. Having one price for a product across all categories and agreements, and with strict management of the change/add/delete process, our analysis for savings validation became possible.

What we considered at SharedClarity is what supply chain executives in other industries would call the total cost of ownership (TCO), which goes far beyond negotiating for lower prices from suppliers. Its definition varies widely across different industries because its basic goal is to look beneath the tip of the iceberg, which is price, to find hidden costs that contribute to the total spend on a given item.

When we look at the total cost of ownership of a product or services, we are considering an overall umbrella performance indicator of *net cost savings* that is common to all other industries—quantifying the bottom line value of the supply chain to the enterprise. When it comes to costs, AHRMM metrics such as *Supply Expense as Percent of Net Patient Revenue*, while valuable, only cover "supply expense" ratios that include other variables (net patient revenue and discharge).

Net cost savings considers both cost increases and decreases, which can be affected by a number of factors, such as price changes from the supplier and level of utilization, yield rates, waste reduction, and repossessing efforts.

For a utilization example, let's say we were considering buying a product that lasts only a week, and it costs $1, but if you pay $2, that product would last a month. Now, you're getting more than four times the use out of it even though the unit cost doubles, so you're actually saving more than 50%.

Net cost savings are best viewed through the lens of the financial statements and budgets: What did it cost to provide that good/service over the past year versus the actual cost today? If I need this product or service to do X, how much did I spend to do that? What was my baseline and what is it now?

Generally, supply chain departments only report the good news. So, as an example, if they take an increase, where the product price goes from $1 to $1.05, they don't report it. But, if they take a decrease, from $1 to $.95, they do. From a financial statement perspective, you need to report everything and see what the bottom line number is. Sometimes, especially in inflationary markets, if you could hold your prices steady or even take only a 5% increase where inflation is 7%, that's still a good thing. Sometimes, your net cost savings goal could be a negative number. What you want to be doing is beating the market and trying to improve your margin—your revenues going up higher than your costs.

Best practices include monthly meetings between supply chain management, finance, and the appropriate budget owners to review recently implemented cost savings projects, especially the ones with significant financial impact, and adjust budgets appropriately. This way, finance and the department budget owners understand what is happening to their budgets in real time, what adjustments can be made, and what they should expect in future financial statements.

An important element of staying ahead of rising costs is not confusing cost avoidance with cost savings. Cost avoidance is the result of avoiding a potential or scheduled future cost increase on a product or service. In supply chain cost avoidance activities, we have to caution against what we call "fool's gold." The following is an example.

A health system is currently paying $1.00 for each pencil it buys. A supplier approaches you and proposes a 10% increase on the per-pencil price to $1.10. The supply chain manager negotiates this proposed increase down to only a 3% increase. So, now, the price becomes $1.03 per pencil. The baseline price is $1.00. Now, they're going to pay $1.03 even though the supplier wanted them to pay $1.10. The accurate way to report this is a $.03 cost *increase* and $.07 in cost avoidance per pencil. GPOs and some health systems could see that as a 7% price reduction, or saving the 7 cents, when all they did was negotiate away 7 cents of the 10-cent increase the supplier wanted. So, if you're talking about budgets and financial statements, the bottom line is your price went from $1 to $1.03. You will run over budget now if you buy too many pencils.

So, what they might call cost savings is them actually accepting a cost increase during that activity, asserting that they have saved 7 cents a pencil when they actually took a 3-cent increase per pencil. Unfortunately, this is a widely accepted method of reporting value and suppliers (and GPOs) know this. So, if suppliers want a 10% increase for example, they will propose a 15% increase. And they will let you negotiate them down to 10%, which is what they wanted in the first place.

The suppliers know that the health systems and GPOs are using cost avoidance as a value metric, so they play the fool's gold game. This practice is also a frequent culprit for finance personnel and department budget owners not having faith in the validity of cost saving reporting of the supply chain department, because the reporting and financial statements don't reconcile.

True cost saving in healthcare takes a lot more work than that, and when we do it well, we conduct it not only in the sourcing process but as part of our EVA strategies as well.

7.4 Missing Category #2: Employee Experience

First, when it comes to this metric, we want to clarify that in our opening example of that longtime health system supply chain leader, we may have been a bit harsh in blaming him for the potential quarter of a billion dollars "he" cost the system over the course of his career. As with all performance improvement opportunities, when we dig a little, we most often find that it is the system enabling, or you might say disabling, the individual that is the problem.

A significant culture shift in effective EVA and strategic sourcing is that the supply chain is seen as a service organization that serves the financial, operational, and clinical needs of the organization. This is why the C-suite, the department chairs, and the physicians all need to be aligned around the supply chain's EVA and strategic sourcing efforts. This is also why employee experience is a vital category of metrics in the supply chain. Successfully employing EVA and strategic sourcing must be deeply tied to culture, and it requires high-level management and communication skills.

AHRMM provides educational and informative opportunities for supply chain professionals, but the AHRMM metrics have neglected to call for measuring and tracking (i.e., improve upon) the skills and knowledge, professional growth, and advancement of supply chain personnel. In every organization, there needs to be a career ladder within and beyond the supply chain for professionals who work in the department. This is crucial in overcoming the Talent Disadvantage Lacuna that prevents health systems from doing effective strategic sourcing.

We believe common metrics in the Employee Experience category should include:

Employee Experience Survey Scores. Employing this metric would include developing such a survey and the educational resources for employees to improve their skills. These would be intertwined with onboarding programs for supply chain professionals who, in addition to working in supply chain experience areas, would also gain knowledge by working within departmental EVA teams and helping to guide their work.

Achievement of Learning Objectives. This metric might include a certain number of hours of continuing education credits, completion of Six Sigma training, obtaining certifications, or even higher learning beyond a bachelor's degree. It also includes experiential learning—for example, rotating into other positions to improve skillsets and/or periodically working for internal customers to better understand their needs.

Succession Planning Process. These metrics would measure the department's and its leadership's goals in a number of areas, including percentage of internal promotions and percentage of key positions with an identified qualified internal successor. This includes developing an internal succession plan with metrics that align with leadership competencies needed in the organization. Meeting these metrics would require close coordination with HR.

Complimentary to the metrics and processes above, health system executive leadership should perform an annual review of supply chain personnel. This would encompass the three processes discussed above wrapped around key supply chain personnel individual performance, looking at each individual in terms of where they lie in the following categories:

- keep/promotable,
- keep/not promotable,
- keep/at risk of leaving,
- don't keep/not promotable.

This process filters the high performers and the promotable from others who may stay onboard or not, and identify those who the system may want to keep, but who they believe may not be satisfied and may look to leave on their own.

7.5 Localizing Strategic Sourcing Changes the Culture Around Costs

If a health system becomes self-reliant and establishes its own supplier contracts and has simplified pricing models versus multiple pricing tiers, the enterprise begins to develop reliable baselines for understanding what their real costs are and what to look for. Even if there are new prices or new SKUs through a change/add/delete process as discussed earlier, they can be effectively managed locally. An example of this might be instituting a process where all change/add/deletes must be reviewed by the VA committee for approval/rejection and can only be input into the Materials Management Information System (MMIS) semiannually.

The simplified pricing that is created by something like our Earned Price Model allows leaders to implement a plan that minimizes product mix shifts. Everyone gets the same price on the same size stent, for example.

So, once you have simplified pricing and rational methods of validating that, the department will have confidence in the knowledge that "We used to pay $1,000 for this thing last year and this year, we're paying $950." This is the point at which finance, the supply chain, and the department budget owner—whether it is oncology or cardiology or the facilities group or marketing or whoever—can take the variables such as patient load shifts and so on and agree upon adjusting their budgets.

If the department was paying $1,000 and now it is paying $950 and it does the same amount of procedures or same amount of volumes, let's say it finds something that saves $250,000 per year. If that quarter million a year isn't considered to be taken out of that department's budget, they could end up with this amount to spend outside their budget needs. At minimum, this saved money should be presented to financial leadership, so they can find the best place for it to support the clinical, financial, and operational needs of the health system. This is one way to demonstrate the benefits of alignment.

In this example, the CEO may step in to say that the $250,000 is not for that department to spend. These savings should be monitored and presented to leadership as soon as they're recognized. Sometimes, they're recognized mid-budget cycle and in the current budget year. When this happens and it's presented in a timely way to financial leadership, a reappropriation might occur that helps another department in ways that benefit the enterprise.

This again represents the activity of a health system that has a culture of alignment, not of individual department self-preservation, which can be seen sometimes. Again, realized cost savings is for the benefit of the entire enterprise, and it goes back to the leadership, so they can effectively figure out how to deploy it within the enterprise where it gets the best ROI. Department leadership and their employees in scenarios managed like this gain credibility because they are saving money regardless of the fact that their budgets may be reappropriated.

The savings from your supply chain cost improvements going back into the organization for the leadership to decide how to best reinvest can be used in ways that drive future savings performance. An example of using it as both a reward and an incentive for future cost reductions could play out in the following scenario. The department might know in advance that they can use 20% of this savings as they deem appropriate within their budget. So you save $250,000, and you get to keep $50,000 for whatever improvements or upgrades you want to make in your department. Maybe a new staff lounge.

This changes the culture of the enterprise and its orientation toward reducing costs.

7.6 Contrasting Cost Savings Validation in the GPO-Led Process

When a GPO is handling the contracts, they also manage the change/add/delete process, and so those cost savings may not be fully recognized when communicated back to the health systems. GPOs just manage them back into their selected tiers. So, the health system is not in control of the cost savings validation. You can't tell how much you're saving on a single product, because it is all lumped in.

Suppliers are also always "changing the packaging." They may change something about the product, whether the price changes or not. This is similar to a candy bar that is at a certain size and a certain price, and suddenly the candy bar has shrunk ever so slightly in size, but the price stays the same. These package change processes have been happening in healthcare for a long time.

With the GPO, validating realized cost savings is likely impossible and not practiced. What is found out, usually during the next budget cycle, is that you're paying more money than you were paying the prior year for the whole package. You hardly know what the cost realities are line by line. And if you were to ask, because of the convoluted processes within the agreements, and the complex tier/price arrangements (which can also change during an agreement term), you may have a difficult time knowing what or how many products with the same item number you're using during a given year.

We should state here that many health system GPO owner members receive an annual distribution—sometimes in dollars and sometimes in consultive services depending on which GPO they may belong to—based in part on the amount of "spend" on the GPO agreements they use and an algorithm that's negotiated into their owner agreement with the GPO.

However, not all GPO agreement users receive this annual distribution, and not all distributions are the same.

The algorithms may be different by owner health system, and generally speaking, "affiliate members" are able to use the agreements, but their share of the distribution will usually go to the owner member they are affiliated with. This is the benefit of an owner working to sign as many affiliate members as possible. GPO owner health system executives may consider these distributions savings in the same way as we've described their health system departmental savings above. This would be very far from true savings, however, because the distributions they receive are based on the contract products they buy that have an administration fee added to them of usually no more than 3% of each agreement dollar they spend. The supplier pays this to the GPO based on their ability to track the health system's spending using invoices they assign to the health system based on purchases.

The fact is, the health system is actually receiving a portion of its own money back, and sometimes up to a year after they spend it. What is ironic about the situation is that GPOs love to market and promote the annual distribution within their membership. Frequently, they turn this transaction into a major event that includes an oversized check, photo shoot, and celebration dinner with senior executives of both organizations.

7.7 Who Has the Reins on the Future of Healthcare Supply Chain?

As we have detailed throughout this book so far, getting at the true measures of cost and quality in healthcare supply chain can be a fuzzy business at best. Depending on the environment your organization operates within, the definitions of terms such as price and cost and value that we think we understood can become blurred or hopelessly convoluted.

Is self-reliance the best option for a brighter future in healthcare supply chain? We answer that question in our final chapter.

As Hungarian-American psychiatrist and author Thomas Stephen Szasz once wrote:

> *"The proverb warns that, 'You should not bite the hand that feeds you.' But maybe you should if it prevents you from feeding yourself."*

Chapter 8

The Future of Healthcare Strategic Sourcing

8.1 Finding Self-Reliance in the Healthcare Supply Chain

Throughout this book so far you may have gotten the impression that we are asking health systems to take the plunge and dump their GPOs. We are not.

We're suggesting something different: First, It is time for us to gain back a meaningful level of self-reliance in the supply chain. We're asking health system leaders to bring pricing and the markets back to rationality by wrestling back control of the value analysis and strategic sourcing processes away from their GPOs and taking them in-house. Health systems need to be self-reliant to ensure their product evaluation and selection processes and sourcing processes together yield the affordability and outcomes results they need to support their enterprise. The GPOs have lost their way in these areas, but because of their diversification, they have the potential to add value in other aspects of the enterprise. Second, we believe the GPO safe harbor should undergo an independent review with a detailed presentation to the appropriate Senate committee for referral on a decision to allow it to continue or be abolished.

We look at it this way: Whoever controls the product-selection process controls the flow of money and quality. As we drove home in our first book, *Implantable Medical Devices and Healthcare Affordability:*

 DOI: 10.4324/9781003495291-9

Exposing the Spiderweb, in the current environment, the suppliers own/influence the product-selection process, physicians are content given the physician preference "veto power," and the GPOs are complicit and have no ability in owning or selecting products. This is especially true of physician preference items, which represent between 40% and 60% of a health system's supply cost (Burns et al., 2018). The enterprise must better position itself to make positive change in affordability and outcomes.

In today's environment, those who are supposed to be your strategic sourcing people are working with the GPOs, and you're trying to manage an irrational market—a situation in which doctors select products but have no financial responsibility for the process, where there's no independent quality and outcome data, where GPOs establish inflated industry-wide pricing benchmarks and forecasts influenced heavily by supplier inputs and empowered by their safe harbor protections, and you're paying a premium for unproven technology. Those variables create an irrational market, which has gotten us to the point of paying up to six times more, at least for implantable medical devices, than other countries, and there are similar situations with pharmaceuticals and capital equipment.

The pandemic laid bare many of the shortcomings of our healthcare supply chain that have been building for decades. Many have blamed these shortcomings on GPOs, who have been the targets of scrutiny by the U.S. Senate repeatedly during the past 20 years, especially around the issue of the 1987 Anti-Kickback Safe Harbors for GPOs. The Medical Device Manufacturers Association testified to a subcommittee of the Senate Judiciary Committee about anticompetitive practices of GPOs as far back as 2006. In 2018, the Association of Physicians and Surgeons asked the Senate Committee on Finance to address the repeal of the GPO and pharmacy benefit managers safe harbors.

And the scrutiny continues today.

In November 2022, several national advocacy groups—including the American Economic Liberties Project (AELP), Practicing Physicians of America, Center for Economic and Policy Research, and Demand Progress Education Fund—sent a detailed, 13-page letter to the Federal Trade Commission (FTC) board asking for an investigation into "the monopolistic middlemen in the healthcare supply chain known as group purchasing organizations (GPOs)." The letter, which was also carbon copied to the Food and Drug Administration, stated, "We believe GPOs play a key and under-appreciated role in fostering and exacerbating shortages and the offshoring of production, while their influence on costs remains chronically under-analyzed" (AELP, 2022).

The letter details how federal agencies, watchdog organizations, and Congress have been investigating and sounding the alarm about GPOs over three decades, and in asking for immediate investigation they stated, "GPOs diminish medical supply market resilience, weaken patient care, and threaten national security." The letter's sponsoring advocacy groups urged the FTC to investigate the following:

- The effects of concentration in the GPO industry and GPOs' impact on competition in the medical supply markets
- GPO concentration and its connection to offshoring of medical supply production
- The effects of GPOs on medical supply prices and reliability of medical supplies
- The effects on medical supply shortages of GPO purchasing and contracting practices
- The frequency of GPOs' use of sole-sourced or exclusive contracts and the effects thereof
- Whether any of these problems would be alleviated by elimination of the anti-kickback statute safe harbor
- Whether the joint purchasing arrangement "antitrust safety zones" should be eliminated.

As of this writing, there is no indication that the FTC has launched such an investigation into major GPOs, but it has added smaller GPOs to its 2023 probes of pharmacy benefit managers (FTC 2023–1, 2023–2). Some moves have been made, however, when it comes to antitrust safety zones.

On February 3, 2022, the AELP reported that the Department of Justice was withdrawing the antitrust safety zones for GPOs. In response, AELP Policy Analyst Sara Sirota stated: "These old and misguided policy statements ushered in the consolidation of medical supply chains under profit-seeking corporations that have reduced patient access to necessary care, made our supply chains brittle, increased wasteful spending, and even threatened national security" (AELP, 2023).

On July 14, 2023, the FTC joined DOJ and withdrew two antitrust policy statements related to enforcement in healthcare markets, one from August 1996 titled, "Statements of Antitrust Enforcement Policy in Health Care," and one from October 2011 titled, "Statement of Antitrust Enforcement Policy Regarding Accountable Care Organizations Participating in the Medicare Shared Savings Program" (FTC 2023–2, 2023).

The announcement stated:

> The FTC has determined that the withdrawal of the two statements is the best course of action for promoting fair competition in health care markets. Much of the statements are outdated and no longer reflect market realities in this important sector of the economy. The Commission's withdrawal follows the Department of Justice's decision to rescind the same statements in February 2023.

While these actions do not necessarily represent a blanket reversal of the safe harbors that GPOs have enjoyed for decades, they are indications that DOJ and FTC are taking a closer look at antitrust law. And according to the FTC's statement: "The Commission will continue its enforcement by evaluating on a case-by-case basis mergers and conduct in health care markets that affect consumers."

Still, we're not saying that you need to disengage from your GPO. Rather, we urge you to take responsibility for your own strategic sourcing. That may mean that your GPO doesn't get an admin fee because you're going to do your own supplier contracts on your own paper, but there are many services your GPO could still provide for you.

We believe the most important element of the term "supply chain management" is that last part—management. A CSCO is a leader and manager who is clearly in charge, with accountability and responsibility for the supply chain within an organization aligned toward EVA and strategic sourcing. In this context, being in charge can't mean outsourcing these processes.

That being said, good managers rely on every resource available, and as a resource operating within the capabilities it excels at, a GPO may be a helpful partner in many ways. GPOs nowadays provide a wide range of services. In fact, GPOs aren't even calling themselves group purchasing organizations anymore.

Vizient is the largest of the four "GPOs" in terms of staffed beds. On the top of its website's home page in large type, Vizient declares itself to be "The nation's leading healthcare performance improvement company." Premier Inc. is arguably the second largest "GPO." On its About page, Premier calls itself "a longtime leader in healthcare improvement," and asserts, "we're developing new ways to revolutionize the industry," emphasizing that they are "maximizing value-based care."

These are some of the lines of business Vizient and Premier Inc. have diversified into the following:

- Consulting in population health and accountable care
- Redesigning approaches to the continuum of care
- Clinical operational and financial performance improvement
- Creating technology platforms for aggregating data and performing analytics for quality improvement activities
- Strategic consulting for medical groups and other physician enterprises
- Enterprise resource planning
- Clinical decision support
- Medical group management
- Managing prescription drug benefits for employees
- Conducting onboarding for physicians and other advanced practice clinicians
- Advocating for health system causes in Congress and federal agencies.

So, let's allow them to help us maximize value-based care for us. Let's have them help improve our performance. Let's let them revolutionize the industry. They reportedly have the ability to serve healthcare organizations very well with the services in the bulleted list above, and their members may be happy with these services. All we are saying is let's take back the things they are not doing well—evidence-based value analysis and effective strategic sourcing. Let's wean ourselves off of reliance on GPOs and wean the GPOs off of their addiction to admin fees. Let them provide some of these new performance improvement services for you for a fee. If the safe harbors that have shielded their precious admin fees are rescinded at some point in the future, you will be prepared, and they will thank you for it. Furthermore, it will foster competition among what we call GPOs and move them in practice into what they have branded themselves as today: performance improvement companies.

8.2 Gaining Control of Industry Priorities

As of this writing, we are still reeling from a pandemic that taught us in healthcare hard lessons about what our priorities should be. In the supply chain, the pandemic initially exposed many weaknesses in product availability and dependency on offshore suppliers, most urgently in lifesaving products that were in critically short supply. These dire shortages of essential medical supplies in the United States caused severe disruptions in medical treatments, resulting in delays, treatment cancellations, and the unfortunate rationing of vital medications. An argument could easily be made that GPOs weren't aware, didn't see it as meaningful, or supported the off-shoring of manufacturing of the products that became so short in supply. Given GPOs' industrywide role in leading strategic sourcing efforts, one could conclude that they were derelict in their duty to build and maintain rational supply markets that would protect their health system members from such a fiasco! Now, they're attempting to clean up the mess that they helped create.

GPOs today speak about having positive impact on supply chain resilience and sustainability. Resilience and sustainability speak to the ability of health systems to gain quick, affordable, and easy access to items that are critically short in supply, yet high in demand. The U.S. Food and Drug Administration (FDA) maintains its Medical Device Shortages List online (U.S. FDA, 2023). At the time of this writing (December 2023), the list of scarce items found there was extensive and included devices and supplies in the following major categories:

- Anesthesiology
- Cardiovascular—circulatory support, and structural and vascular devices
- Cardiac diagnostic and monitoring products
- Dialysis-related products
- General hospital and plastic surgery devices
- Radiological devices
- Certain ventilation-related products.

From that list it appears we have a long way to go toward the supply chain resilience and sustainability the GPOs are promising.

Health systems over the past few decades have delegated (and funded) industry strategic thought leadership and priority setting over to GPOs. The following is an example of where that leads.

In late September 2023, a $10.3 million joint venture was announced between Premier, DeRoyal Industries, and 34 of Premier's member health systems to create a healthcare products manufacturing facility in Powell, Tennessee. In announcing the deal, Premier President Michael J. Alkire stated, "A strong workforce, expanding infrastructure, and robust business environment make Tennessee an ideal location for the production of isolation gowns—a vital product for our nation's healthcare providers" (Premier, 2023)

Isolation gowns: A vital product!? You mean versus new drugs, and more ventilators and other lifesaving equipment!? In the wake of the pandemic, Premier's big solution they and 34 of their member health systems are spending time and resources on is isolation gowns? Nobody died because of a shortage of isolation gowns.

Not to belabor the point, but there is no doubt that DeRoyal Inc. is a strong partner in this endeavor, and we can understand the doors that open when a company such as DeRoyal invests in this way with a GPO, so nobody should blame DeRoyal for seizing this opportunity. It is GPOs that market themselves as being vital to health systems' ability to thrive and serve patients. So, when they deliver a partnership for isolation gowns as evidence of creating resilience, we in the industry should seriously question them.

If in the wake of the pandemic we brought together health system thought leaders such as Mayo Clinic, Johns Hopkins, and Cleveland Clinic as examples to discuss their most critical supply chain needs going forward, we believe strongly they would say that manufacturing isolation gowns doesn't meet their idea of top priorities.

We hope that others, possibly a more forward-looking GPO, are working on creating sustainability for products that are more critical to saving lives, especially in the unsettling healthcare industry reality in which large health systems have accelerated outsourcing supply chain management operations and strategic leadership to third parties and GPOs. In doing this, they are not just allowing their supply chain functions to be outsourced on a health system level. They are literally outsourcing the priorities of the entire healthcare industry out of the hands of the people who know them best—health system leaders.

Self-reliance doesn't just mean having the headcount and doing all of the daily blocking and tackling work involved in running the supply chain. It also means leading the vision and the strategy, and that has reverberations throughout the industry.

8.3 Beating Back the Effects of the Lacuna Triangle

We have felt enough pain in healthcare supply chain in the United States in recent years. We as supply chain and health system leaders can use newly found self-reliance to get to work on reversing the deleterious effects of the Lacuna Triangle. Building evidence-based value analysis and effective

Figure 8.1 The Effects of the Lacuna Triangle

strategic sourcing into the healthcare supply chain means aggressively confronting the effects of the Lacuna Triangle—oligopolies, irrational pricing, and irrational markets—by addressing each of the Lacunas. See Exhibit 8.1.

8.4 SCM Talent Lacuna: Addressing the Disadvantages with Development

We start with developing supply chain management talent. This is going to take a long view because currently strategic sourcing as we're presenting it in this book is underrepresented by professionals within healthcare with the skills and experience required to make the broad changes that will close this lacuna. This is in part because of the influence of GPOs over the past few decades, who also lack the necessary talent and the common practice of hiring and promoting within healthcare versus infusing talent from other industries that can have a wider skillset.

Again, healthcare SCM/strategic sourcing roles and responsibilities are "watered down" compared to other industries because of GPOs owning a large part of those processes, roles, and responsibilities. We need to give our strategic sourcing professionals opportunities to develop and lead cross functional teams, develop/align/influence people around strategies, negotiate, and develop a wide internal and external industry network. These experiences and skills are career launchpads transferable into many other promotional opportunities.

We also can begin to make our health system supply chains into career launchpads in large part by bringing in the talent from outside of healthcare, especially in branded health systems such as Kaiser, Mayo, Duke, Cleveland Clinic, and Hopkins, which can hit the ground running, creating sweeping changes and reengineering supply chain processes that close this lacuna. Then, by disengaging from the GPO, the strategic sourcing professional can be seen as the primary supply chain influencer through physician, nurse, supplier, and C-suite relationships.

We need to create effective onboarding programs for supply chain personnel starting on the ground floor, using examples from other industries like the Conagra Brands example in Chapter 4. This is a good first step in recruiting top talent from leading supply chain graduate programs and moving them up a logical career ladder.

In organizations in which a high percentage of people in the supply chain have come laterally from other areas of the organization—clinical or nonclinical—leadership should determine whether the percentage needs to be tilted more toward people from outside of healthcare for the benefit of external experience. We can intentionally create whatever ratio leadership feels is appropriate in the interest of infusing "new blood" and fresh perspectives into the supply chain.

In the interest of attracting top talent into the supply chain, leadership also needs to consider what the career ladder for supply chain personnel is within the hospital or health system. Can someone starting out in supply chain aspire to someday rise to the highest levels of the company? Given the complexity, interconnectedness, and importance of the supply chain from a financial perspective, someone with deep knowledge of the health system supply chain with the right breadth and length of experience should be excellent COO or even CEO material. There are examples of supply chain leaders moving into CEO positions at hospitals and health systems in other countries, as we mentioned in Chapter 4.

Does your organization project the alignment and culture that top supply chain talent is looking for in an employer? Are the CEO, COO, CFO, CMO, and CNO appropriately aligned around supply chain success so that as necessary changes in supply chain and strategic sourcing are executed and change pushback within the "tribe" starts to surface to the C-suite level, the alignment won't be broken? Will you know you can count on support from the top as a supply chain leader in this organization when necessary change is warranted? Or, do you believe they will cave to the pressure, as happens in most health systems today, which means failure for not only the supply chain leader but also for the reputational value of the position.

Another aspect of change pushback in loosening the bonds around the Lacuna Triangle and perhaps a more stringent test on an organization's alignment around supply chain is physician preference.

8.5 Changing the "Why" in PPI

Physician preference as a label for product selection need not have a negative connotation in healthcare. To get physician preference to having a positive connotation, we have to change the *why* around physician preference.

The old *why* evokes responses such as "I prefer this product and insist we use it because (insert any reason, a few of which we have listed below)"

> " I've been using it since med school."
>
> "the manufacturer trained me in it and keeps me up to date on new entrants in the product pipeline."
>
> "I get paid speaking engagements related to promoting this product at major national conferences."
>
> "the manufacturer provides me with real-time tech support in surgery if I get in a bind."

The new *why* elicits responses such as "I prefer this product because . . ."

> "our Orthopedics Department has thoroughly researched the quality of this device and found that it outperforms all similar devices on the market."
>
> "the manufacturer is piloting research on its next generation device in our facilities."
>
> "this device has saved our health system more than $350,000 annually compared to similar devices we used in the past."

"we negotiated product technical support with the sup-
plier/manufacturer as part of our contract."

"patient outcomes and satisfaction scores have improved
significantly as a result of this product."

Getting to the new why means ensuring that the EVA process is structured as we have laid out so far in this book: a physician-led effort with
finance, clinical, supply chain, and the C-suite represented. Any new
items that come into a hospital or health system's supply chain go into
that EVA process within the appropriate department or business unit,
and they are benchmarked against existing similar products.

These items then become part of the cost-validation process. Contract
negotiators need to be wary, especially with multiple-line suppliers, that
suppliers are not giving discounts on high-utilization items but making
up the discounts by upselling other items.

Physician preference is heavily influenced by vendors. The EVA/strategic
sourcing model when conducted as we have described in this book should
naturally take the supplier out of its predominant role in shaping physician
preference. It empowers the clinician with information on costs, which is
usually the missing piece—and a vital one organizationally speaking—in
how physicians come to prefer one manufacturer's product over another's.

Several of the high-performing supply chains in healthcare have
explicit expectations of suppliers and a process for vetting them. An
example of this is Mayo Clinic, which was singled out in 2022 along with
Intermountain Health Care as a "Supply Chain Master" in its annual
Gartner Healthcare Supply Chain Top 25. This designation is placed on
these supply chain leaders for having attained Top 5 composite scores in
the annual Top 25 for at least seven of the past 10 years (Gartner, 2022).

If you are a supplier, you don't just walk into one of the locations of the
world's largest integrated group practice and start talking with doctors.
No, they have specific sign-in locations especially for you, and you can
find out where they are at the first place you will likely go to—the Supplier
Information portion of the Mayo Clinic website (Mayo Clinic, 2023).

At that site, you will find information on:

■ Mayo Clinic's Supplier Guidelines
■ Supplier Resources, which include several areas of resources suppli-
  ers must review:
  – Authentication and Registration
    • Current Mayo Clinic locations and address list (Excel and
      Word)
    • Supplier and Sales Representative Code of Conduct (PDF)

- Supplier Briefings (PDF)
- Code of Ethics and Conduct: Integrity and Compliance Program (PDF)
- Anti-Retaliation Policy (PDF)
  - Equal Employment Opportunity and Affirmative Action
    - Mayo Clinic Equal Employment Opportunity and Affirmative Action Policy (PDF)
  - Quote Template
    - Quote template letter (PDF)
    - Quote template instructions (PDF)
    - Quote template (Excel)
  - Third Party Risk Assessment
    - Architecture diagram template (Visio and PDF)
    - Software Bill of Materials (Excel)
    - Subcontractor Request Form for Third Party Risk Management
- ▪ Supplier Diversity Program
  - Supplier Diversity Registration Portal.

Just from this list one can deduce that there is a robust program for vetting suppliers. In fact, its vendor onboarding process also includes verifying company information, validating tax information for accurate IRS reporting, identifying minority suppliers, and verifying that the supplier has not been sanctioned by any regulatory agencies.

With regard to suppliers visiting a Mayo Clinic location, even if they have successfully navigated the onboarding process, they must have an appointment and sign in at one of the designated sign-in locations. According to the organization. "Contacting or visiting Mayo physicians or staff without an appointment, or coming on campus without registering, can result in your sales privileges being temporarily or permanently revoked."

When dealing with the physician preference quandary, questions like the following are key: How does a health system minimize the physician conflict of interest and having relationships with your suppliers? How do you get more independent data to make better decisions? How do you change the market to pay for performance and results versus just paying for the newest shiny object?

Fully developing relationships of value with physicians is key to eliminating physician conflict of interest with suppliers. Leadership should demonstrate that they care about what their physicians care about, and are actively assisting them in reaching their professional goals and ambitions, aligning with the physicians "where they are" at all levels of the health system.

This can include supporting research and independent studies. Developing data capture and analytics capabilities within the health system can assist in these initiatives. Also, data collaboratives could be established with other health systems such that independent studies could be performed that are supported by the physicians and the health systems and findings could be shared. This health system should be able and willing to provide value to the physicians who deliver value to the health system.

8.6 Alignment Lacuna: EVA and Strategic Sourcing Drive the Organization in One Direction

As supply chain professionals who have implemented EVA and strategic sourcing programs, we know that it has the power to align an organization like perhaps nothing else can. As we have pointed out, these are organizational initiatives that begin with the leadership and staff of both clinical and nonclinical departments focusing on improving both quality and costs.

Alignment is the pivotal issue of the Lacuna Triangle, because it is the overall driver in ridding the organization of the other two lacunas that prevent effective EVA and strategic sourcing:

- The participation of supply chain personnel requires that you have highly competent and trained staff that have an organization-wide appreciation for the financial, operational, and clinical/nonclinical needs of the organization and are not simply order takers.
- Physicians and other clinical personnel with decision-making responsibility for product selection and use are part of a collaborative process of selecting those products, and thus, they are armed with performance and pricing data that come together in consolidation, standardization, and rationalization.

CSCOs who can drive alignment by having a complete understanding of the level of resources, talent, and internal goals and objectives required to create a plan to move forward. Next, we need to make implementation of EVA and strategic sourcing a priority with alignment of the entire C-suite, including the CSCO and their staff. This is the only way to drive alignment throughout the enterprise that will be robust enough to overcome the disadvantages created by the level of resources, talent, and internal strategic focus that suppliers are able to bring to bear on health systems.

8.7 Moving Forward with Strategic Sourcing

There is a huge amount of chicken-before-the-egg/cart-before-the-horse (or whatever analogy you prefer) going on in our healthcare supply chain Lacuna Triangle. You can't have top-tier supply chain talent if the talent from another organization is running much of the show that should be run by SCM personnel and those staff are relegated to order taking. You can't have evidence-based value analysis and strategic sourcing if physicians are allowed to simply choose products, instead of being lead influencers of those efforts, where they understand the financial and quality costs of their decisions. And last of all, you can't have either of those things without alignment throughout the organization.

If we are going to tackle the issues of high costs and poor outcomes in the U.S. healthcare system relative to the rest of the world, it needs to start with healthcare systems taking back control of the supply chain and as an enterprise addressing the lacunas that limit their ability to become a global leader in cost and outcomes.

Teaching institutions in healthcare need to expand their healthcare management curricula with a focus on grooming the next generation of self-reliant future CSCOs. Healthcare organizations must provide the processes and resources to recruit, onboard, and prepare incoming supply chain associates for a well-rounded knowledge base that results in the skillsets we need for evidence-based value analysis and effective strategic sourcing. At the same time, in the supply chain, they need to balance their ratios of legacy "insider" personnel for that experience edge in working with internal departmental stakeholders and "outsider" personnel for fresh perspectives in operating in a self-reliant environment.

Healthcare organizations need to change the view of physician preference as a category and redefine physician preference by changing the "why" of PPI, as we presented earlier in this chapter. We can change physician preference from an assumption, or opinion, of value and quality to proof of value and quality by putting physicians and other clinicians in charge of our value analysis processes and giving them the data and analytics tools they need to do the job right. Once they are empowered to use science to understand the true cost and outcome consequences of the products and services they are recommending, the entire equation changes, and the positive effects downstream on our strategic sourcing efforts become enormous.

None of this happens without alignment throughout the organization on EVA and strategic sourcing. In an aligned environment, supply chain leaders are elevated from being mere order takers in these processes, and physicians and departmental budget owners are working together gaining intelligence on how products perform both from financial and outcome perspectives so they can standardize, rationalize, and consolidate. Supply chain personnel are then using that data to inform and leverage their strategic sourcing efforts.

The suppliers and their complicit GPOs currently own the product selection process. That means together they control what happens with cost and quality—as we have pointed out throughout this book—the two greatest areas of failure in the U.S. healthcare system. If health systems were already self-reliant and followed best practice strategic sourcing processes, they would have rational supply markets and would not be experiencing the depth of the resilience/product availability and affordability issues they are currently facing.

So the answer is not more expenditure. As we pointed out in the beginning of this book, the U.S. healthcare system is responsible for 42% of the world's healthcare spending and more than half of the total spending among high-income countries. We need to begin fixing the root causes of the problem instead of continuing to throw more money at it.

The goal of all this effort toward self-reliance is to find the optimal, aligned solution to meet the financial, operational, and clinical (and nonclinical) needs of the enterprise. If there ever comes a time when all of us in the U.S. healthcare system are doing this, we will see that the percentage of GDP in healthcare spending starts moving downward, and our healthcare outcomes begin to improve in relation to other developed countries in the world.

References

American Economic Liberties Project (AELP). (February 22, 2022). *Advocates urge the FTC to investigate GPOs' impacts on drug, medical equipment shortages and rising healthcare costs.* www.economicliberties.us/press-release/advocates-urge-the-ftc-to-investigate-gpos-impacts-on-drug-medical-equipment-shortages-and-rising-healthcare-costs Letter; www.economicliberties.us/wp-content/uploads/2022/11/2022-11-22-AELP-FTC-6B-GPO-Letter-Final.pdf

American Economic Liberties Project (AELP). (February 6, 2023). *DOJ signals more aggressive stance on GPOs.* www.economicliberties.us/press-release/doj-signals-more-aggressive-stance-on-gpos/

Burns, L., Housman, M. G., Booth, R. E., & Koenig, A. M. (2018). Physician preference items: What factors matter to surgeons? Does the vendor matter? *Medical Devices: Evidence and Research, 11,* 39–49.

Federal Trade Commission (FTC, 2023–1). (June 8, 2023). *FTC further expands inquiry into prescription drug middlemen industry practices.* www.ftc.gov/news-events/news/press-releases/2023/06/ftc-further-expands-inquiry-prescription-drug-middlemen-industry-practices

Federal Trade Commission (FTC, 2023–2). (July 14, 2023). *Federal trade commission withdraws health care enforcement policy statements.* www.ftc.gov/news-events/news/press-releases/2023/07/federal-trade-commission-withdraws-health-care-enforcement-policy-statements

Gartner. (2022). *Healthcare supply chain top 25 for 2022.* www.gartner.com/en/supply-chain/trends/gartner-healthcare-supply-chain-top-25

Mayo Clinic. (2023). *About mayo clinic: Supplier information.* https://www.mayoclinic.org/about-mayo-clinic/supplier-information

Premier. (September 22, 2023). *Governor Lee, Commissioner McWhorter announce DePre to establish headquarters and manufacturing operations in Knox County* (Press Release). https://premierinc.com/newsroom/press-releases/governor-lee-commissioner-mcwhorter-announce-depre-to-establish-headquarters-and-manufacturing-operations-in-knox-county

U.S. Food & Drug Administration. (November 27, 2023). *Medical device shortages list.* www.fda.gov/medical-devices/medical-device-supply-chain-and-shortages/medical-device-shortages-list

Index

Note: Page numbers in *italics* indicate a figure and page numbers in **bold** indicate a table on the corresponding page.

Printed in the United States
by Baker & Taylor Publisher Services